The Voice as an
INSTRUMENT

Second Edition

Raymond Rizzo

Bobbs-Merrill Educational Publishing

Indianapolis

Copyright © 1978 by the Bobbs-Merrill Company, Inc.
Printed in the United States of America

The Bobbs-Merrill Company, Inc.
4300 West 62nd Street
Indianapolis, Indiana 46268

Second Edition
First Printing 1978

Library of Congress Cataloging in Publication Data

Rizzo, Raymond.
    The voice as an instrument.

    Includes index.
    1. Voice culture.   I. Title.
[PN4162.R55   1977]   808.5   77-9433
ISBN 0-672-61407-3

CONTENTS

PREFACE

This second edition of *The Voice as an Instrument* has provided me with a rare opportunity to remake one of my progeny. It is entirely because of the many helpful reports from the field that I have made additions, which consist sometimes of fuller explanations, but most frequently of more and more exercises. I have always seen the request for more exercises as a very good sign, for my basic thesis, that skills must be acquired and mastered through experience, remains, like the basic text, intact.

This new edition, therefore, contains a fuller explanation of the anatomy of the speech mechanism; more relaxation exercises; a song exercise for the lips and the tongue; a fuller introduction to the International Phonetic Alphabet (IPA), and new exercises for each sound in the IPA; an explanation of the diacritical marks, and new exercises stressing vocabulary building for each sound; and a new section of selected readings.

My acknowledgments for this second edition are few and brief, but nonetheless gratefully made. To the memory of Susan Steell, a fine actress and teacher, I still find I owe most of what I know about speech and its importance. I wish to thank the following members of John Jay College of Criminal Justice: Professor Flora Rheta Schreiber for reading the chapter on anatomy; Mr. Austin Fowler for reading the many new exercises on phonetics; Professor Georgiana Peacher for her insights; and Mrs. Florence Grossman and the Faculty Services for typing Chapter One. I also wish to thank Skidmore College and its library for making available to me needed books for research when I was working in Saratoga Springs during the summer. To my wife, I offer my deep appreciation for her generous gift of editing.

RAYMOND RIZZO
John Jay College of Criminal Justice, New York City

EXERCISES

The Voice as an
INSTRUMENT

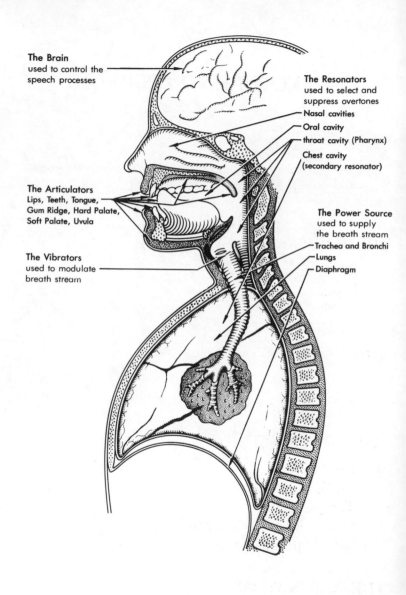

The Brain
used to control the
speech processes

The Resonators
used to select and
suppress overtones
Nasal cavities
Oral cavity
throat cavity (Pharynx)
Chest cavity
(secondary resonator)

The Articulators
Lips, Teeth, Tongue,
Gum Ridge, Hard Palate,
Soft Palate, Uvula

The Power Source
used to supply
the breath stream
Trachea and Bronchi
Lungs
Diaphragm

The Vibrators
used to modulate
breath stream

Chart 1. The Voice and its parts. (Courtesy Bell Laboratories)

THE VOICE AND ITS PARTS

The voice as an instrument is divided into four distinct parts:
the power source, the vibrators, the articulators, and the resonators.

THE POWER SOURCE

Diaphragm
Lungs
Trachea and bronchi

THE VIBRATORS

Larynx
Vocal cords

THE ARTICULATORS

Lips
Teeth
Tongue
Gum ridge and hard palate
Soft palate and uvula

THE RESONATORS

Nasal cavities
Oral cavity
Throat cavity (pharynx)
Chest cavity (secondary resonator)

1

You Speak with
a Musical Instrument

$\mathcal{A}$ few years ago, while directing a production of Schiller's *Mary Stuart* at a girls' college near New York City, I was listening to a senior speech major race through a piece of complex exposition which, by her speed, she was rendering unintelligible.

"No, no, no!" I called to her from the darkened theatre.

"I know," she said, smiling graciously, "I'm going too fast!"

"You are indeed. Much too fast!"

"They've been telling me that ever since I was a freshman here," she sighed.

"And what did they suggest you do about it?"

"They said I should *slow down.*"

For years, incredible as it may seem, the speech department had been advising her, "Slower! Go Slower!" without ever telling her how to go about going slower.

Now, at least part of the blame for this regrettable situation is the girl's, for never finding out for herself how to go about slowing down. And I would like to ask you, right now, not to accept any statement in this text without some intellectual curiosity, some questioning. Ask yourself why each exercise is

3

presented, what error in speech it is designed to correct; ask how you can correct your own speech deficiencies (and everyone has some speech deficiencies). Question your instructor; question yourself. The improvement of speech is not an operation which takes place on an anesthetized body. It is a matter of self-discipline which involves hard work and the fullest consciousness and self-awareness possible.

If you were to use any machine, from a motorcycle to a church organ, a knowledge of how its parts work would help you to use it to better advantage. This is especially true when the machine is not working well. Your knowledge could help you to find the trouble and get the machine running smoothly again.

The instrument that is your voice is a complex machine, as seen in Chart 1. Acquiring knowledge of its various parts and how they are related to one another will help you to use it more efficiently. Remember, this particular machine can't be returned to the factory for a replacement. A special technician can always be called in to help, but you are the best possible person to keep it working smoothly.

It is important that you realize, first of all, that you are speaking with a musical instrument. Think about this statement, because if you can refute it (and in twenty years of teaching I have never heard it refuted), I cannot teach you. However, if you are merely unsure that the voice is a musical instrument, you will logically ask, "But how does it work? What are its parts?" In this chapter, we shall discuss the various parts of the "musical instrument," your voice.

THE POWER SOURCE

Diaphragm

The *diaphragm* is a huge muscle that separates the lungs from the digestive organs. Its main function, from the birth cry to the death rattle, is to pump air out of the lungs. When you

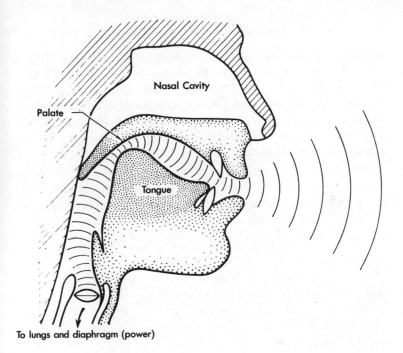

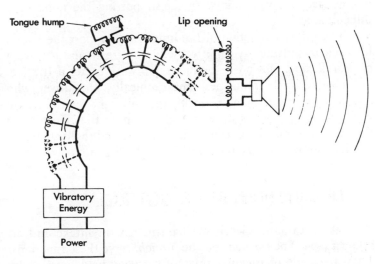

FIG. 2. Speech Chain. (Courtesy Bell Laboratories)

exhale, your diaphragm pushes up into your chest cavity like a big hand forcing air out of the lungs. When the diaphragm descends again, it leaves behind the emptied lung sacs which are quickly refilled by air pressure. Although an inhalation is often noticeable because the stomach protrudes, this is not true for everyone. In Chapter Two you will find exercises to strengthen the diaphragm and to help you achieve efficient breathing.

Lungs

The *lungs* are shaped like triangles, narrow on top, wide at the bottom. For this reason, diaphragmatic breathing is more efficient than chest breathing, where you must lift your heavy collar bones to get air into the small area at the top of the lungs—a waste of energy rewarded by a minimum of air. Diaphragmatic breathing involves stomach protrusion rather than chest lifting. For really efficient breathing, watch a baby when it is howling, or a well-trained singer supporting the notes of a difficult aria.

The primary function of the lungs is to support the body's life cycle by putting oxygen into the blood stream and removing carbon dioxide. Obviously the lungs will work better if they are not clogged with impurities, but, ironically, the driver who orders the air filter changed on his car will light up a cigarette while doing so. Poor posture may also hamper the efficiency of the lungs; cramped lungs can't inhale deeply and shallow breathing does not provide the body with enough oxygen.

Trachea and Bronchi

Like a car, the speech mechanism has an intake and an exhaust pipe. The *trachea* and the *bronchi* serve these functions. They are made of irregular rings of cartilage held together by muscular fibers, tissues, and mucous membranes. The trachea starts at the base of the larynx and branches off into the right and left bronchi with tubes that spread into the lungs. The cartilages of the trachea and the bronchi are highly elastic, but may become calcified in advanced age.

THE VIBRATORS

Larynx

The *larynx*, or voice box which houses the vocal cords, is at the upper part of the trachea and the root of the tongue. It is made of cartilages which are connected by ligaments and moved by numerous muscles. Before puberty, the larynx of the male differs little from that of the female. After puberty, however, it nearly doubles in size, and the Adam's apple becomes prominent in the center of the throat. The increase in size, of course, is what produces the deepened tones of the mature, male voice. In the female, there is a slight increase in the size of the larynx after puberty.

Vocal Cords

The *vocal cords* are the actual sound producers. The sound they make is amplified first by the larynx, which houses them. The vocal cords consist of two strong bands of yellow elastic tissue which are stretched across the larynx. They are controlled by muscles that turn the larynx so that the opening between them can be made narrow for a high note, or wide for breathing during heavy exercise.

Slightly above the main vocal cords are the false vocal cords. These consist of two thick folds of mucous membrane covering a short band of tissue. Although they can make sounds, they are called "false" because they are responsible for the "falsetto" notes of the voice.

The vocal cords are subject to the law of physics which

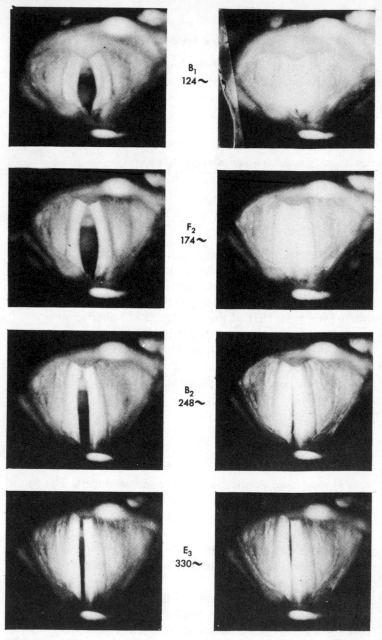

FIG. 3. High-speed motion pictures of the human vocal cords: open and closed position of vocal cords at 124, 174, 248 and 330 cycles. (Courtesy Bell Laboratories)

states that the shorter and narrower the vibrating object, the higher the rate of vibration. A wire stretched between two poles will vibrate at a higher rate when the tension is increased on the wire, because the thickness of the wire is decreased. If the length of wire is decreased, the pitch also rises. The shorter the length, the higher the pitch or rate of vibration. The longer the length, the lower the pitch or rate of vibration. In a church organ, the short pipes produce the high notes and the long pipes produce the low notes.

In Chapter 13 you will learn the Rocket Exercise, in which you glide down through the falsetto range to the lowest note you can sound. At this time you will be able to determine, with your instructor's help, whether your voice is working at the best possible pitch.

THE ARTICULATORS

The raw sounds leaving the larynx would remain animal grunts and growls if it were not for the *articulators*: the tongue, lips, teeth, gum ridge and hard palate, soft palate and uvula. Before considering each articulator, you should examine your mouth and its parts.

Close your eyes and place the tip of your tongue against your upper teeth where they meet the gums. Rub the tip of your tongue back and forth to make sure it is at the right place. Now press the tip of the tongue hard against that point and then move it backwards and upwards. Repeat this a few times. You should have felt a bump. That bump is the gum ridge. As the tongue continues on past the gum ridge, it discovers that the mouth arches into a high curve. You should feel a sense of the vastness of your mouth. This high curve or arch is called the hard palate. As the tongue continues, it descends into the soft palate at the rear of the mouth.

Repeat the journey a few times, using a mirror. Examine what you have just discovered with your tongue. Notice the little piece of flesh hanging in the back of the mouth. That is the part of the soft palate that is called the uvula. We can now describe each articulator, in turn, and the sounds it helps produce.

Lips

Vigorous *lip* action, avoiding exaggeration, will help you speak with clarity. The next time you go to the theater or the movies, watch the lips of the leading actors, or on television watch the lips of the newscasters on national broadcasts.

Teeth

The *teeth* play an important role in supplying the tongue and lips with a surface to play against in the making of sounds. Your front teeth are especially essential, for certain sounds cannot be made without them. *S* is a sound that relies not only on the presence of all the front teeth, but also on their proper alignment; gaps between the front teeth will result in a leaky *s* that is more like *sh*.

Tongue

The *tongue* is a muscle that forms, in combination with the teeth, the sounds called the lingua-dentals. The voiced *th*, as found in the word *that*, and the unvoiced *th*, as found in the word *think*, are the only two lingua-dental sounds. (*Voiced* means simply that the vocal cords are vibrating. See Chapter 5.)

The movements of the tongue are numerous and complicated. The muscles involved easily get set in bad habits. One of the most difficult tasks that a speech student is called on to perform is to change poor tongue habits.

In Chapter Three, you will find exercises for strengthening tongue muscles. A sluggish tongue is responsible for most mumbling and slurring. Remember Hamlet's advice to the actors: "Speak the speech, I pray you . . . trippingly on the tongue!"

Gum Ridge and Hard Palate

The *hard palate* separates the mouth cavity from the nasal cavity above it. Years ago, people born with a break in the hard palate (called a cleft palate) had to spend their lives honking every time they spoke. Today, thanks to modern surgery, no one needs to suffer from this speech impediment.

Soft Palate and Uvula

The *soft palate*, or the *velum*, is composed of muscles which reach into the back of the mouth. The soft palate, as you discovered on your exploratory trip, ends in a small piece of flesh called the uvula that hangs in the back of the mouth.

Without the uvula you could never blow air through the nose or mouth with any degree of intensity. It acts as a valve that directs the air flow; when it is pressed down against the tongue, it effectively prevents the mouth from receiving any air. This happens automatically when you blow your nose. The reverse happens when you blow up a balloon; the uvula blocks the nasal passage by flipping against the back of the throat, directing all the air to flow into and out of the mouth. In rare cases, when the uvula is sluggish, the result is a nasal voice sounding somewhat like the voice of a person with a cleft palate. In such instances, a speech therapist may prescribe blowing up balloons to strengthen the pharyngeal muscles that control the uvula.

THE RESONATORS

All musical instruments need *resonators* to boost the volume of their vibrations. The vibrations of the vocal cords also need boosters. The body's voice instrument has three *primary* resonators: the cavities of the nose, the mouth, and the throat; and one *secondary* resonator, the chest.

Nasal Cavities

The *nose*, or septum, is composed of bone and cartilage surrounding the large cavities of the sinuses. The amount of resonance that takes place in the nose is regulated by the action of the pharyngeal muscles.

Oral Cavity

The *mouth* as resonator is best thought of as a megaphone. Take a large piece of paper and roll it so that one end is narrow and the other end is wide. When you talk into the narrow end, your voice is magnified or amplified. The mouth works exactly like this loudspeaker.

Throat Cavity (Pharynx)

The *pharynx*, or throat cavity, is the first resonator to receive sound from the vocal cords. The pharynx has a set of constricting muscles which line the sides of the throat. These muscles can squeeze the walls of the throat around the soft palate so that the entrance to the nasal cavity is open or closed, and can also control the quality of sound issuing from the vocal cords.

Chest Cavity

The *chest*, a secondary resonator, responds sympathetically to the vibrations of the vocal cords. Sympathetic vibrations occur when the frequency (rate of vibration) of the vocal cords is the same as the resonant frequency of the cavity.

The size of the resonator is one factor in determining the resonant frequency. The rule is, as with the larynx, the larger the resonator, the lower the frequency. The thick strings of the bass violin, which make low notes, need the large box of the bass violin to support the sympathetic vibrations. Violin strings stretched across a bass violin would get very little sympathetic vibratory help from the big box.

Proper posture is also important, not only for efficient breathing, but also to make the chest cavity a better sounding board.

Let us now assume that you have a good idea of how your musical instrument works—in theory.

THE IMPORTANCE OF PRACTICE

What would you think of a music teacher who placed the following ad in the papers: "Revolutionary New Method! Learn to play the violin WITHOUT PRACTICING! *No exercises!* Results guaranteed. Call Professor Mountebank at . . ."?

The professor might get a few calls from the kind of person who would buy the Brooklyn Bridge. But most of us would stay far away from him. Why then do students approach a speech class with the attitude that they can learn to play their voices proficiently without doing the exercises? Because, you may be thinking, while you cannot play the violin, you can already speak and have been doing so for as long as you can remember. If there *is* anything you do not know about playing your voice, you're going to have to be shown.

The aim of this book is to show you. Its material is divided into three parts. The first part (Chapters Two and Three) will help you to strengthen, relax, and make flexible your mouth, lips, and tongue. The second (Chapters Five to Eleven) will teach you the proper pronunciation of the sounds of General American Speech, so that you can speak with greater clarity. The third (Chapter Thirteen) will teach you to speak to better effect, in a well-modulated and interesting voice, a voice that has range of pitch, fullness of tone, ease of production. But to speak with clarity and control of your instrument, you must exercise. You will be asked to practice, and practice, and practice. You will spend your time not learning the anatomy of the speaking mechanism but doing the exercises. You will have to learn to read the phonetic alphabet of speech notation as you would have to learn to read musical notation, and then you will have to practice, practice, and practice playing these "notes." You will not learn phonetic transcription. That and the anatomy quizzes can be reserved for the future speech therapist.

You are going to learn to speak the speech "trippingly on the tongue," but first you must do what Demosthenes did to develop a superb speaking voice: practice. I am not going to ask you to put pebbles into your mouth, but I hope at this juncture you are asking yourself why Demosthenes *did* put pebbles into his mouth. Think. Perhaps your answer is that he put pebbles into his mouth so that he would be certain that if he could speak clearly with pebbles in his mouth, then he could speak clearly once they were taken out again. In a sense you are right. Demosthenes used the pebbles to strengthen his articulators. His tongue had to lift the pebbles; his lips and cheeks had to hold the pebbles; and of course when he declaimed on the seashore, pitting his voice against the roar of the surf, his diaphragm was strengthened and his vocal range increased as his vocal cords were exercised day after day. In the end he became the greatest orator among a nation of great orators.

In the past twenty years I have seen what appeared to be miracles worked in students. I have seen students freed from the curses of mumbling, slurring, poorly pitched and inarticulate speech, speech made unintelligible by heavy regionalisms. I have had students with tiny voices of cripplingly limited range turn into interesting speakers, and monotone speakers learn to speak with variety. It is immensely gratifying to turn a student burdened by any of these deficiencies into a speaker of clearly enunciated, well-projected, and well-modulated English. But I have never seen it done without the same sort of hard drill work performed by Eliza Doolittle in *My Fair Lady*.

In our drill work you will need one basic tool, a mirror. The mirror is necessary to help you see what you are doing with your lips and tongue as you work. Make sure you are provided with one before you begin.

By this time you are possibly frightened at the prospect of doing so many exercises, the importance of which I have stressed again and again. Why, you ask, should *you* exercise? Is your speech really *that* bad?

Your problem may be a lazy tongue and lips. It may be your pitch, your volume, or your speed of delivery. It may be your breathing. In many of my students it is any of these things, as well as their diction.

Once a student came to me after our first class meeting of the semester.

"Professor, I *have* to do something about my speech," he said.

Then he told me about a wonderful weekend with a Vassar beauty whom he much admired, who at their parting advised him to read the play *Pygmalion*. He was determined never to be so embarrassed, so *discriminated against*, again.

Granted that the young lady was a heartless snob, who wants to let himself in for an unnecessary snub? In a sense the young man was lucky. Bad diction is like bad breath—and the offender is often the last to know. The young man of the Vassar weekend was luckier than another student I knew, a brilliant young business major with an A average who had been sent by his college placement bureau to a bluc-chip corporation as a sure prospect for executive training. Eventually the corporation informed the placement bureau that they regretted being unable to use the young man because "his speech is so very poor that it would jar our corporate family life."

This student had been shortchanged by his college. He had been put through a speech course that was in reality a course in public speaking, or the communication of ideas, with no attention paid to his speaking instrument.

To get ready for an important social or business encounter, you groom yourself carefully. Your hair is neat, your teeth are brushed, your shoes are polished; you have given thought to the clothes you are wearing. But more important than the clothes you will wear will be the words you speak, and many a promising job applicant has altered a favorable impression by opening his or her mouth.

Before we go on to the exercises, I'd like to ask you one more question. From what root does the word *student* derive? And what does the root mean? No, it does not mean "to study." The Latin *studeo* means, "I strive after." Perhaps you realize that the purpose of this chapter has been to motivate you to work. I would like your being a student of speech to mean that in reality you strive after good speech, for if you strive after it strongly enough, you will have it.

Education cannot happen without a change taking place in the one who is educated. You will enter this course with one voice, will work on the exercises, and will emerge with another voice. Desire better speech and it will be yours.

This is one of the most personal courses you will ever take. What comes out of your mouth is a projection of you. It is important that you have a healthy self-love and therefore a strong desire to improve. If you cannot love yourself, you cannot love your neighbor.

Finally, where it has been said that the pen is mightier than the sword, I would like to add that the spoken word is mightier than the written one. More people were swayed by the spell of Hitler's speeches than by *Mein Kampf*. His voice mesmerized a nation. We can thank God that Winston Churchill had superior oratorical powers to spur and encourage another nation to withstand Hitler. History is full of great leaders who had a master's command of their musical instruments: Franklin Roosevelt, Benito Mussolini, John F. Kennedy, Fidel Castro, Mayor Fiorello LaGuardia, and the list stretches on. Out of charity I shall not name the equally long list of recent failures, the hopefuls who did not have the magnetism or the delivery to capture the people's imagination and votes.

I don't want to seem guilty of Willy Lomanism by promising success through better speech alone. There has to be an educated mind behind the educated speech mechanism. But, as Nicholas Murray Butler, a great educator and past President of Columbia University, once said, "You can identify an educated man by three distinctive hallmarks, his ability to think, his ability to write, and his ability to speak."

And now, enough of motivation. Let's get on with the lessons.

2

Relaxation

*L*ife is full of tensions, and Americans annually depend on millions of pounds of pills to relieve these tensions. We have pills for relaxation, pills to make us sleep, and pills to ease allergies and other psychosomatic symptoms, not to speak of the alcoholic method for letting go. We all know we ought to relax, but most of us, like the girl of the first chapter who knew she should speak slower, don't know how to go about it.

TENSENESS AND VOICE PITCH

A tense body cannot house a relaxed speaking voice, and it is impossible to speak well unless the voice is relaxed. It is a natural law of physics that the more tightly a wire is stretched, the higher the pitch of its sound when plucked. The same principle applies to your voice. When your vocal cords, along with

17

the rest of your body, are tightened, your voice is raised in pitch; and what is worse, it lacks resonance and carrying power.

Each person has his own personal optimum pitch level, where his voice will be at its full resonance and beauty. (In Chapter Thirteen you will learn to find this level and to speak at it.) Most individuals speak habitually at a pitch well above their optimum pitch levels, just as most habitually walk around with a posture that could be improved. How pleasing, the sight of a person with an erect carriage and the sound of a beautifully controlled voice!

It is important in doing the relaxation exercises given below that you not only learn to relax but learn to distinguish when your body is in a relaxed state and when it is not. You can then be on guard against a tightened voice and the ills that go with it.

For these relaxation exercises, I hope you have the convenience of a room in which you can be isolated, if only for a short time. It is possible, but much more difficult, to relax in a crowded room.

EXERCISE 1

Recognizing and Relieving Tension

In a darkened room, place a mat or a blanket on the floor. Wearing as little clothing as possible, and removing all bindings such as belts, tight collars, and constricting underclothes, do the following:

1. Lie on your back on the mat or blanket.

2. Curl the toes of your right foot as if you were going to pick up something with them. Close them as tightly as possible. Now quickly release them. What you have just experienced is tension and its absence.

3. Slowly proceed up the entire body, tightening and releasing in succession the foot muscles, calf muscles, and thigh

muscles of first the right leg, then the left leg. Do the same with the buttocks, the right hand, the right arm, and the left hand and arm. Follow the same procedure with abdomen and chest. Contort the face into a tight grimace and release. If the entire procedure is done slowly and repeatedly, you will learn both how to recognize tension and how to release it.

The next exercise is based on an ancient principle of Yoga: breathing is vital to living. You can go without water, food, and sleep far more easily than without air. If, therefore, you can control your breathing, you are winning control of a vital life function. If you can slow your breathing perceptibly, you can slow the metabolism of the body.

EXERCISE 2
Basic Yoga

1. Lie on the mat on your back under the same conditions as in Exercise 1.

2. Put your left hand on your abdomen, below the rib cage.

3. Blocking the right nostril with the right thumb, inhale slowly through your left nostril, keeping your mouth shut. As you inhale, you should feel your stomach *pushed out* by your diaphragm. Time your inhalation so that it lasts while you slowly count six.

4. Blocking both nostrils with right thumb and index finger, hold your breath and continue your slow count for as long as possible. A count of twelve is good; advanced students can increase the count to twenty or twenty-four.

5. Removing thumb from right nostril begin to exhale slowly through your right nostril only, as your diaphragm gradu-

ally pulls your abdomen down and in. Let the air out as slowly as possible to the same count of six.

6. When all the air is expelled, sharply pull the diaphragm into the rib cage as far as possible.

7. Repeat Steps 1 through 6 five or six times.

While breathing deeply as you perform the preceding exercise, you may respond with an elevation of the rib cage in the style of a West Point cadet. You must remember that in proper, normal breathing, the diaphragm pushes the abdomen *out* when you inhale, and pulls it *in* when you exhale. The reason for this is simple. The lungs are triangles with their bases at the bottom. It is therefore uneconomical to lift the entire rib cage in order to take a deep breath, for you are expending much energy to fill a tiny space. Diaphragmatic breathing, on the other hand, opens up the base of the triangle, and helps the lungs to work most efficiently with least expenditure of energy. Remember, when you take a deep breath, not to pull back your shoulders and raise your rib cage, but rather to feel your abdomen protrude. Leave your shoulders and ribs in the normal position.

EXERCISE 3

The Diaphragmatic Lift

In Exercise 2 you felt your diaphragm expand and contract while you were lying on your back. Now you will experience diaphragmatic action in a standing position. Ancient Yoga texts promised eternal life to devout practitioners of this exercise. I hope you will settle for the immediate rewards of relaxation, vitality, and diaphragmatic control.

Avoid this particular exercise if you have had any heart trouble, stomach disorders, or a chronic appendix. Never do it immediately after meals. The deep breathing brought about by the diaphragmatic action in the following exercise should never be violent or abrupt in either the contraction (exhalation) or the expansion (inhalation). Go slowly.

1. From a standing position, spread your feet about twelve inches apart.

2. Bend your body slightly forward and place your hands on the upper, inner part of your thighs.

3. Exhale slowly and completely until you feel that you have emptied your lungs. Your stomach is pulled up into the rib cage, forming a hollow curve.

4. Press down on your right hand while letting it slide slowly down along your inner thigh.

5. When your right hand reaches slightly above the knee, start to press down on your left hand for a second slow slide.

6. Continue this cycle of right and left hand presses along the inner thighs until you need to inhale.

7. Stop pressing your thighs and inhale slowly.

This exercise is an excellent start at getting control of the diaphragm, *an absolute essential in speech work*. Notice how relaxed you feel after doing five or six deep presses and inhalations. A bonus is the flattening effects of the exercise on the abdominal walls.

EXERCISE 4

Rag Doll

1. Unfettered by tight clothing and with your shoes removed, stand with your legs apart, but not too far, so that you have a good sense of balance.

2. Think of a puppet that has had its strings cut—it collapses. In the same way drop your body from the waist so that it folds over, your head hangs limp, and your arms dangle to the ground.

3. If you are doing the exercise in class, the instructor can test your relaxation by lifting and then dropping your arm. If it falls and swings like a pendulum, you are truly relaxed. If it "assists" the instructor by shooting up as he lifts it, or if it remains in the lifted position without dropping, you are tense. Another sign of tension is a stiff neck, which thrusts the head forward. Your head should hang like a ball at the end of the spinal column.

4. If you are doing the exercise in class, the instructor should have you try dropping over several times, to be sure no one is cheating by slowly lowering his body into position. The body must *fall* from the waist, collapsing toward the ground.

5. From the collapsed position, now raise the torso slowly, remembering that the arms and head are still not energized. When you are standing upright, the arms will fall naturally to the sides and the head will be hanging forward on the chest, a dead weight unsupported by any muscle. The instructor can check for relaxation as in Step 3.

6. Now rotate the head in as wide a circle as possible. The head should revolve like a ball on a string. Do not raise the shoulders. Be sure the head passes over the right shoulder, the back, the left shoulder, and comes back to a forward position on the chest.

7. Reverse the headroll, doing it in the opposite direction.

8. Repeat Steps 6 and 7 several times.

9. If you have come this far successfully, your neck muscles, your face muscles, and your vocal cords are relaxed. You are now ready to try sounding a relaxed vocal instrument.

10. Slowly raise the head, and while doing so, simulate a yawn
    —or really yawn—and at the same time sound an "ah."
    Open your mouth as wide as possible. Repeat several
    times, taking a deep breath with the diaphragm before
    beginning each "ah." Letting your breath out slowly, sus-
    tain each "ah" for as long as you can. You have just heard
    the most relaxed sound you can make; repeat it so that
    you can remember what it feels like to make it. If you
    have been working correctly, you have also heard your
    voice at its optimum pitch level, the pitch at which you
    should habitually speak. Try to carry this resonant tone
    into your everyday speech. (In Chapter Thirteen another
    exercise is given to help you achieve this resonant tone.)

11. After repeating the "ah" sound six to ten times, add an
    "mmmmmm" to its end. Slowly close the mouth as you
    form the "m" until the lips are quite closed. Push with
    your diaphragm so that a good air flow is passing over your
    vocal cords. If you can feel your lips vibrate and tingle,
    this is a good sign of facial, as well as tonal relaxation. Tak-
    ing a deep diaphragmatic breath and slowly closing the
    mouth to form the "m," repeat "ah . . . .
    mmmmmmmm" six times.

It would be difficult to find the acting company, movie lot,
or television studio where an actor is not using the Rag Doll to
relax before a performance, for actors know that not only the
voice, but the entire body, must be relaxed if they are to be at
their best.

EXERCISE 5

The Lion Posture

This exercise is one of contrasts. It will help you to recognize tension when it attacks the face or throat. Tension in these
areas can lead to vocal fatigue or a very sore throat after a short
period of speaking. Use this exercise before a public speaking

occasion and you will discover, with gratitude, that the muscles of the throat are relaxed and ready to work smoothly.

1. Sit on a chair. Or, if you prefer, squat on the floor, resting your buttocks on your heels.

2. Place your hands on your knees, palms down.

3. Slowly inhale and hold your breath, as in Exercise 2.

4. Then, as you slowly exhale, stick out your tongue as if you were trying to expel it from your body. Keep your mouth and eyes wide open. If your tongue is really extended, you will feel the resulting tension in your neck muscles.

5. Hold this ferocious position for as long as you can; then relax. (If you don't believe you look ferocious, use a mirror and you will see why this is called the Lion Posture.) Contrast the feeling of relaxation with that of tension.

6. Repeat this exercise five or six times.
Remember that the facial mask and mouth form a megaphone which will work best when free from tension.

EXERCISE 6
The Circle

This exercise can be performed only in a group.

1. The group forms a circle with each member facing left.

2. Reach out and take hold of the shoulders of the person in front of you. Press your thumbs into the base of his neck and use your fingers to hold the neck muscles that flow into the shoulders. Slowly and carefully massage the

shoulder and neck muscles of the person in front of you, applying pressure on the back of the neck with your thumbs, and the neck muscles with your fingers. (If your own massage is too strong, then tell your masseuse to ease up).

3. Lift your head slowly back while you take a slow inhalation.

4. As massaging continues, slowly yawn and vocalize a loud, relaxed *ahhhhhh*.

5. When your breath is expired, slowly lower your head.

6. Repeat five times. Wait for everyone to finish.

7. About face and follow Steps 2 through 6 on your new subject.

8. After the last five inhalations and exhalations, drop hands and face the center of the circle.

9. Do five or six slow headrolls as you did in the Rag Doll (Exercise 4).

EXERCISE 7
Push-Pull

In this group exercise you will use your voice while other muscles are in a state of great tension. The theory is that the tension, being in the other muscles, will leave the vocal cords relaxed.

1. Each person faces a partner.

2. Extend your arms and press your palms against your partner's.

3. Take a deep inhalation.

4. Push against your partner's hands with slow but steady pressure.

5. As you do this, sound an *eeeeeeeeeee*, until your breath is exhausted.

6. If your breath is exhausted but your partner is still going, then continue to push until your partner is through.

7. Repeat steps 2 through 6 five times.

8. Change your grip now so that your hands are interlocked in preparation for a pull.

9. Take a deep breath.

10. Slowly pull on your partner's hands as you sound a wide open *ahhhhhhhhhhhhhhhhhhhhhhh*.

11. Repeat five times.

EXERCISE 8

Marching

The purpose of this next group exercise is to vocalize while moving. Lift your feet high for the march, swinging your arms vigorously. Have fun! Keep time! Sing as loudly as you can, enjoying the freedom and looseness of your voice. Don't worry about whether you sound like a professional singer.

1. Form a wide circle.

2. Leave enough space between participants so that all can march vigorously without hitting anyone.

3. March, singing:

> Mine eyes have seen the glory of the coming of the Lord!
> He has trampled out the vintage where the grapes of
>   wrath are stored;
> He has loosed the fateful lightning of his terrible swift
>   sword;
> His truth is marching on!
> Glory, glory, hallelujah!
> Glory, glory, hallelujah!
> Glory, glory, hallelujah!
> His truth is marching on!

Continue to practice the relaxation exercises, and remember to use your developing ability to control tension and relaxation as you begin, in the following chapters, to exercise the more particularized speech areas.

3

Lip and Tongue Exercises for Better Articulation

The world seems much smaller today than it did even a few years ago—and it is growing still smaller! The ease of jet airplane travel, and more importantly, the standardization of entertainment that began with the movie and continues with television, are making us more homogeneous in speech throughout the nation. Regionalisms are no longer so snugly tucked away under the Mason-Dixon line, in the northeastern corner of the United States, or within the confines of large cities like New York. Today mobile Americans are moving from one part of the country to another in increasing numbers. The same speech is uttered by the actor in Hollywood and the newscaster in New York, and it is this same speech that large corporations with offices all over the country desire for their executives, so that they can be easily shifted about. Hence the popularity and practicality of what has come to be known as General American Speech, which is, very broadly, speech as it is heard throughout America, excluding the South and the Northeast.

GENERAL AMERICAN SPEECH

The idea that the time approaches when all over the country educated Americans will be pronouncing a standardized language scarcely differing in Texas, Wyoming, Georgia, and Massachusetts, is viewed with mixed feelings. Many of us will mourn the passing of speech regionalisms, much as we already regret the loss of the handmade shoe, dress, or piece of furniture, while at the same time we enjoy the standardized quality and lowered price of the mass-produced article. Nevertheless, the tendency in this country is very strong towards the development and acceptance of General American Speech. Besides the impetus given it by mass communication media and the corporation families, the graduate speech departments throughout the country have adopted and are teaching it; and the speech graduates who leave these schools are a great leavening agent.

For this reason people planning certain careers cannot afford to ignore General American Speech. In the twenty years that I have been teaching it, I have received many letters from former students with excerpts like the following.

> I have just accepted a lucrative job opportunity in the public relations field. Besides having offered me a nice salary, they have agreed to finance half the expense of my law school education at night. In evaluating me as a prospective employee for their company, they told me that one of the contributing factors was the fact that the personnel committee could not detect a New York accent in my speech. When I heard this fact, I could not help thinking how beneficial and important your speech course was to me. Right then and there I realized that articulation is of equal importance with self-expression.

> I want to thank you personally for the improvement in my speech brought about by your emphasis on diction. At present I am a graduate teaching assistant in English at a midwestern University; since I arrived at the university, I have met students from all parts of the country. When I mention that I

was born and raised in New York City, they remark, "I'm surprised you don't have an accent." One graduate assistant in his second year took me for a native of Milwaukee! Naturally my improved diction will enhance my teaching career; an English teacher who cannot speak clearly and distinctly does not belong in front of the classroom.

The decision whether to speak General American Speech is yours to make. It is the speech that I will be teaching when we get to phonetics and diction, and if you study this course, you *can* end up speaking it. On the other hand, if you want to preserve your regionalisms, I suggest you use the course to develop your ear so that at least you can hear and pronounce the differences. Then you will always be in control of your speech, and you can work for greater clarity of articulation within the framework of the regionalisms that you have chosen.

Good speech must begin with the speaker's ability to *hear* himself and his own speech defects. You must become a dynamic rather than a passive listener, analyzing as you hear. Listening assumes a major role in speech-course work. During any class you will spend most of the hour listening. As your ear sharpens, you will begin to listen outside of class. And once you can associate the correct sounds with the symbols of the IPA and can pronounce these sounds accurately because you know where to place your lips and tongue, you are on your way to good speech that is unalterably yours.

But any changes must be made carefully to avoid phoniness. Shaw pointed out this trap in his preface to *Pygmalion:*

> But the thing has to be done scientifically, or the last state of the aspirant may be worse than the first. An honest and natural slum dialect is more tolerable than the attempt of a phonetically untaught person to imitate the vulgar dialect of the golf club . . . .*

Remember not to assume that because you have been speaking English since you were a child, you have mastered its sounds.

---

* G. B. Shaw, *Selected Plays* (New York: Dodd, Mead, 1948), I, 194–95.

Approach your language freshly, as if it were a foreign tongue, for when you attempt to produce a General American sound that is not in your habitual repertory of sounds, you will feel that you *are* speaking a foreign tongue. It will not be easy to alter old speech patterns. If you have always, for instance, said *jist* for *just* you will have to learn to hear yourself saying *jist* before you begin to find out how to alter the sound. The following steps are involved in a change in articulation.

1. Learn how to relax.

2. Exercise your lips and tongue to the point where they can respond easily to instruction as to their proper placement.

3. Learn to associate sound and its written symbols with the placement of tongue and lips necessary to produce it. You must drill as any foreign-language student does in mastering a foreign tongue.

Step 1 has been treated in Chapter Two. The present chapter will undertake to teach Step 2.

Remember that the following exercises are comparable to the fingering exercises the pianist or organist must perform on his instrument to master the keyboard. They must be done daily or the muscles will not be trained. Unless the lips and tongue, your articulators, really move when you speak, clear, precise speech is impossible.

While practicing the exercises, you should exaggerate and overpronounce. It is not intended that you reproduce the sounds in this way in your everyday speech or in public speaking. A scale played for practice on the piano will have an emphasis not used in the glissando of a piano concerto. In speech, too, we want the natural, fluent flow of the glissando—but only with the discipline of the oft-repeated scale behind it.

The following exercises are purposely composed of nonsense syllables. Since you will be using a mirror to watch your lips and tongue at work, it is important at first to use speech materials that will not distract you.

These exercises aim to help you learn how to move your

lips in order to overcome slurring, mumbling, and speaking too fast. Exaggerate lip movement. Use your mirror to watch lip and tongue movement. Warning: relax as you work. Do not contort your face or neck.

EXERCISE 9
For the Lips

1. Exaggerate to extreme as you repeat twenty times:

> eeeeeee—aahhhhhhhh—oooooooooo
> (Lips drawn back—"eeeee," mouth opened wide—"ahhhh," lips protruding and almost closed—"ooooo.")

2. First, pronounce the consonant with closed or nearly closed lips, and then reproduce the "ahhhh" sound of Step 1 with a fully opened and relaxed mouth in the following combinations (repeat each line four times):

> fah, fah, fah, fah, vah, vah, vah, vah
> pah, pah, pah, pah, bah, bah, bah, bah
> mah, mah, mah, mah, nah, nah, nah, nah

3. Moving the lips from a closed position to an exaggerated smile position, and remembering to move nothing but the lips, repeat rapidly four times each:

> me-me-me-me
> pree-pree-pree-pree
> wee-wee-wee-wee

4. Whisper the following words three times each to exercise lazy lips:

> ontological, anachronistically, ecumenical, superfluity, impracticable, lexicographer, irremediable, posthumously, im-

possibility, impenetrable, schizophrenic, voluptuousness, existentialism, ignominiously, irrevocable, philosophical, polysyllabic, disingenuousness, incalculable, preposterous, antidisestablishmentarianism, supercalifragilisticexpialido-cious.

(As the mouth receives very small vibrations from the vocal cords when you whisper, your lips must work exaggeratedly. Remember, whispering is a strain on vocal cords. If you feel any hoarseness, stop. When you have a sore throat, do not resort to whispering, for it is more taxing than normal speech.)

5. The following verses are to be read slowly, aloud, and with exaggerated mouth action:

a.   I
On a little piece of wood,
Mr. Spikky Sparrow stood;
Mrs. Sparrow sat close by,
A-making of an insect pie,
For her little children five,
In the nest and all alive,
Singing with a cheerful smile
To amuse them all the while,
      Twikky wikky wikky wee,
      Wikky bikky twikky tee,
      Spikky bikky bee!

II
Mrs. Spikky Sparrow said,
'Spikky, darling, in my head
Many thoughts of trouble come,
Like to flies upon a plum.
All last night, among the trees,
I heard you cough, I heard you sneeze;
And, thought I, it's come to that
Because he does not wear a hat!

Chippy wippy sikky tee,
Bikky wikky tikky mee,
Spikky chippy wee!

III

'Not that you are growing old,
But the nights are growing cold.
No one stays out all night long
Without a hat: I'm sure it's wrong!'
Mr. Spikky said, 'How kind,
Dear! you are, to speak your mind!
All your life I wish you luck!
You are, you are, a lovely duck!
    Witchy witchy witchy wee,
    Twitchy witchy witchy bee,
    Tikky tikky tee!

IV

'I was also sad and thinking,
When one day I saw you winking,
And I heard you sniffle-snuffle,
And I saw your feathers ruffle;
To myself I sadly said,
She's neuralgia in her head!
That dear head has nothing on it!
Ought she not to wear a bonnet?
    Witchy kitchy kitchy wee,
    Spikky wikky mikky bee,
    Chippy wippy chee?'

V

'Let us both fly up to town;
There I'll buy you such a gown!
Which, completely in the fashion,
You shall tie a sky-blue sash on.
And a pair of slippers neat,
To fit your darling little feet,
So that you will look and feel
Quite galloobious and genteel!

Jikky wikky bikky see,
Chicky bikky wikky bee,
  Twicky witchy wee!'

VI

So they both to London went,
Alighting on the Monument;
Whence they flew down swiftly—pop,
Into Moses' wholesale shop;
There they bought a hat and bonnet,
And a gown with spots upon it,
A satin sash of Cloxam blue,
And a pair of slippers too.
  Zikky wikky mikky bee,
  Witchy witchy mitchy kee,
    Sikky tikky wec!

VII

Then when so completely drest,
Back they flew, and reached their nest.
Their children cried, 'O Ma and Pa!
How truly beautiful you are!'
Said they, 'We trust that cold or pain
We shall never feel again;
While, perched on tree, or house, or steeple,
We now shall look like other people.
  'Witchy witchy witchy wee,
  'Twikky mikky bikky bee,
    'Zikky sikky tee!'

—EDWARD LEAR
Mr. and Mrs. Spikky Sparrow

b.
I am the very model of a modern Major-General,
I've information vegetable, animal, and mineral,
I know the kings of England, and I quote the fights
  historical,

From Marathon to Waterloo, in order categorical;
I'm very well acquainted too with matters mathematical,
I understand equations, both the simple and quadratical,
About binomial theorem I'm teeming with a lot o'
        news—
With many cheerful facts about the square of the hy-
        potenuse.

I'm very good at integral and differential calculus,
I know the scientific names of beings animalculous;
In short, in matters vegetable, animal, and mineral,
I am the very model of a modern Major-General.

I know our mythic history, King Arthur's and Sir Cara-
        doc's,
I answer hard acrostics, I've a pretty taste for paradox,
I quote in elegiacs all the crimes of Heliogabalus,
In conics I can floor peculiarities parabolous.
I can tell undoubted Raphaels from Gerard Dows and
        Zoffanies,
I know the croaking chorus from the *Frogs* of Aris-
        tophanes,
Then I can hum a fugue of which I've heard the music's
        din afore,
And whistle all the airs from that infernal nonsense
        Pinafore.

Then I can write a washing bill in Babylonic cuneiform,
And tell you every detail of Caractacus's uniform;
In short, in matters vegetable, animal, and mineral,
I am the very model of a modern Major-General.

In fact, when I know what is meant by "mamelon" and
        "ravelin,"
When I can tell at sight a chassepôt rifle from a
        javelin,
When such affairs as sorties and surprises I'm more
        wary at,

And when I know precisely what is meant by "com-
    missariat,"
When I have learnt what progress has been made in
    modern gunnery,
When I know more of tactics than a novice in a nun-
    nery;
In short, when've a smattering of elemental strategy,
You'll say a better Major-General has never *sat* a gee—

For my military knowledge, though I'm plucky and
    adventury,
Has only been brought down to the beginning of the
    century;
But still in matters vegetable, animal, and mineral,
I am the very model of a modern Major-General.

—W. S. GILBERT
The Pirates of Penzance

c.

'Twas brillig, and the slithy toves
Did gyre and gimble in the wabe:
All mimsy were the borogoves,
And the mome raths outgrabe.

'Beware the Jabberwock, my son!
The jaws that bite, the claws that catch!
Beware the Jubjub bird, and shun
The frumious Bandersnatch!'

He took his vorpal sword in hand:
Long time the manxome foe he sought—
So rested he by the Tumtum tree,
And stood awhile in thought.

And, as in uffish thought he stood,
The Jabberwock, with eyes of flame,

Came whiffling through the tulgey wood,
And burbled as it came!

One, two! One, two! And through and through
The vorpal blade went snicker-snack!
He left it dead, and with its head
He went galumphing back.

'And hast thou slain the Jabberwock?
Come to my arms, my beamish boy!
O frabjous day! Calooh! Callay!'
He chortled in his joy.

'Twas brillig, and the slithy toves
Did gyre and gimble in the wabe:
All mimsy were the borogoves,
And the mome raths outgrabe.

                  —LEWIS CARROLL
                  Jabberwocky

d.   I

On the Coast of Coromandel
Where the early pumpkins blow,
In the middle of the woods
Lived the Yonghy-Bonghy-Bò.
Two old chairs, and half a candle,
One old jug without a handle,—
These were all his worldly goods,
In the middle of the woods,
These were all the worldly goods,
Of the Yonghy-Bonghy-Bò,
Of the Yonghy-Bonghy-Bò.

II

Once, among the Bong-trees walking
Where the early pumpkins blow,
To a little heap of stones

Came the Yonghy-Bonghy-Bò.
There he heard a Lady talking,
To some milk-white Hens of Dorking,—
' 'Tis the Lady Jingly Jones!
On that little heap of stones
Sits the Lady Jingly Jones!'
Said the Yonghy-Bonghy-Bò,
Said the Yonghy-Bonghy-Bò.

III

'Lady Jingly! Lady Jingly!
  Sitting where the pumpkins blow,
    Will you come and be my wife?'
  Said the Yonghy-Bonghy-Bò.
'I am tired of living singly,—
On this coast so wild and shingly,—
    I'm a-weary of my life;
    If you'll come and be my wife,
    Quite serene would be my life!'
  Said the Yonghy-Bonghy-Bò,
  Said the Yonghy-Bonghy-Bò.

IV

'On this Coast of Coromandel,
  Shrimps and watercresses grow,
    Prawns are plentiful and cheap,'
  Said the Yonghy-Bonghy-Bò.
'You shall have my chairs and candle,
And my jug without a handle!
    Gaze upon the rolling deep
    (Fish is plentiful and cheap)
    As the sea, my love is deep!'
  Said the Yonghy-Bonghy-Bò,
  Said the Yonghy-Bonghy-Bò.

V

Lady Jingly answered sadly,
  And her tears began to flow,—

'Your proposal comes too late,
  Mr. Yonghy-Bonghy-Bò!
I would be your wife most gladly!'
(Here she twirled her fingers madly,)
    'But in England I've a mate!
    Yes! you've asked me far too late,
    For in England I've a mate,
    Mr. Yonghy-Bonghy-Bò!
    Mr. Yonghy-Bonghy-Bò!'

VI

'Mr. Jones (his name is Handel,—
Handel Jones, Esquire, & Co.)
  Dorking fowls delights to send,
Mr. Yonghy-Bonghy-Bò!
    Keep, oh, keep your chairs and candle,
    And your jug without a handle,—
    I can merely be your friend!
    Should my Jones more Dorkings send,
    I will give you three, my friend!
    Mr. Yonghy-Bonghy-Bò!
    Mr. Yonghy-Bonghy-Bò!

VII

'Though you've such a tiny body,
  And your head so large doth grow,—
  Though your hat may blow away,
Mr. Yonghy-Bonghy-Bò!
Though you're such a Hoddy Doddy,
Yet I wish that I could modi-
    fy the words I needs must say!
    Will you please to go away?
    That is all I have to say,
Mr. Yonghy-Bonghy-Bò!
Mr. Yonghy-Bonghy-Bò!'

VIII

Down the slippery slopes of Myrtle,
  Where the early pumpkins blow,

> To the calm and silent sea
> Fled the Yonghy-Bonghy-Bò.
> There, beyond the Bay of Gurtle,
> Lay a large and lively Turtle.
>> 'You're the Cove,' he said, 'for me;
>> On your back beyond the sea,
>> Turtle, you shall carry me!'
> Said the Yonghy-Bonghy-Bò,
> Said the Yonghy-Bonghy-Bò.

—EDWARD LEAR
from The Courtship of the Yonghy-Bonghy-Bò

Using your mirror, you are about to encounter a shy creature, a muscle not used in the light of day, a creature that has almost certainly, until this moment, led an independent life. It is not accustomed to being dominated, but is a coward and will respond quickly to firm discipline. Without a disciplined tongue that is active and responsive in its movement, clearness of speech is impossible. You want energetic lip and tongue movement, however, only if it results in a clear but not overarticulated speech. Now begin to tame that independent creature, remembering that it is a coward and that you must rule over it in your house of speech.

EXERCISE 10
For the Tongue

1. Open your mouth as widely as possible.

2. *Point* your tongue in the *center* of your mouth opening. (The tongue at first will have a tendency to flatten. Make sure it is not flat, but rounded and pointed; think of gathering, or pulling it together.)

3. With the *tip* of the tongue, and the tip only, touch the *out-side* of your upper lip, the outside of your lower lip, then the left and right sides of the mouth.

4. Repeat for one minute. Keep your mouth open; if it starts to close, hold it open with your hand.

(Note: If you are one of those rare persons who cannot do this exercise because your tongue is literally tied to the bottom of your mouth, perhaps your frenum should be cut to allow the tongue to move more freely. Ask your speech instructor to recommend a good speech clinic where you can be seen by a doctor. Difficulty with consonant sounds in which the tongue has to reach the roof of the mouth is also sometimes due to a frenum that should be cut.)

EXERCISE 11

For the Tongue

1. Looking into the mirror, stretch your tongue until it can almost touch the tip of your nose. One person in a thousand can touch the nose, so don't worry if you don't succeed. *Try* to touch the tip of your nose.

2. Pull the tongue back into the mouth.

3. Again extend the tongue, this time as far down the chin as possible.

4. Repeat Steps 1 through 3 as fast as you can until you grow tired, but do them for at least a minute. Have a handkerchief ready to wipe away any excess moisture when you have finished.

EXERCISE 12
For the Tongue

This is an isometric exercise. Remember Demosthenes, who worked his tongue against pebbles? You will work yours against the roof of your mouth.

1. Keeping your mouth closed, press the tip of your tongue against the roof of your mouth.

2. Start to curl the tongue *slowly*, over the roof of the mouth, pressing up all the time as hard as possible. Once you hit the soft palate, go back to where the teeth meet the gums.

3. Repeat at first for a minute, increasing the time gradually to two minutes. If you are working correctly, you will feel a burning sensation in your tongue.

EXERCISE 13
For the Tongue

1. Open your mouth as widely as possible. Form a large circle with your lips. Now with the tip of your tongue, ride around the rim of the mouth in one direction for one minute, slowly at first, and then faster.

2. Reverse the sweep of your tongue, riding with the tip around your mouth in the opposite direction for one minute, slowly and then faster.

A good variation on following your tongue in the mirror is to close your eyes and follow the movement in your mind. You might try this method with the following exercise, in which the mouth is not so wide open as in the preceding exercises.

EXERCISE 14

Vocalization

1. Repeat each line rapidly four times:

> tee-lee tee-lee tee-lee tee-lee
> lee-ree lee-ree lee-ree lee-ree
> tah-tay-tee-tah tah-tay-tee-tah tah-tay-tee-tah
>   tah-tay-tee-tah
> lah-lay-lee-lah lah-lay-lee-lah lah-lay-lee-lah
>   lah-lay-lee-lah

Notice how your tongue has to move. Go slowly at first; then increase the tempo until you speak the sounds "trippingly on the tongue."

2. Repeat each line rapidly four times:

> tah tah tah tah
> dah dah dah dah
> lah lah lah lah
> sah sah sah sah
> zah zah zah zah

3. Read in an exaggerated articulation, moving the jaw as if you were chewing an apple, and speaking loudly and slowly:

a. The Seven young Parrots had not gone far, when they saw a tree with a single Cherry on it, which the oldest Parrot picked instantly, but the other six, being extremely hungry, tried to get it also. On which all the Seven began to fight, and they scuffled,

> and huffled,
> and ruffled,
> and shuffled,
> and puffled,

and muffled,
and buffled,
and duffled,
and fluffled,
and guffled,
and bruffled, and

screamed, and shrieked, and squealed, and squeaked, and clawed, and snapped, and bit, and bumped, and thumped, and dumped, and flumped each other, till they were all torn into little bits. . . . One said this, and another said that, and while they were all quarrelling the Frog hopped away. And when they saw that he was gone, they began to chatter- clatter,

blatter-platter,
patter-blatter,
matter-clatter,
flatter-quatter, more violently

than ever. . . . So after a time [they] said to each other, 'Beyond all doubt this beast must be a Plum-pudding Flea!' On which they incautiously began to sing aloud,

'Plum-pudding Flea,
Plum-pudding Flea,
Wherever you be,
O come to our tree,
And listen, O listen, O listen to me!'

—EDWARD LEAR
*The History of the Seven Families
of The Lake Pipple–Popple*

b. Polly, Dolly, Kate and Molly,
All are filled with pride and folly.
Polly tattles, Dolly wriggles,
Katy rattles, Molly giggles;

Whoe'er knew such constant rattling,
Wriggling, giggling, noise and tattling?

—MOTHER GOOSE

4. Say each tongue twister three times as rapidly as possible:

    a. She makes a proper cup of coffee in a copper coffee pot.
    b. A box of biscuits, a box of mixed biscuits, and a biscuit mixer.
    c. She sells seashells by the seashore.
    d. Sinful Caesar sipped his snifter.
    e. Unique New York.
    f. Rubber buggy bumpers.
    g. Watch the whacky wristwatch.
    h. The big black bug bled black blood.
    i. Lemon liniment.
    j. Strange strategic statistics.
    k. Six thick thistle sticks.
    l. Purple pickle percolator.

5. In the next selection, don't try for speed; clarity is your goal. Read through silently first to get the sense; then read aloud. And have fun!

Oh! my name is John Wellington Wells,
I'm a dealer in magic and spells,
    In blessings and curses
    And ever-filled purses,
In prophecies, witches, and knells.

If you want a proud foe to "make tracks"—
If you'd melt a rich uncle in wax—
    You've but to look in
    On our resident Djinn,
Number seventy, Simmery Axe!

We've a first-class assortment of magic;
    And for raising a posthumous shade

With effects that are comic or tragic
   There's no cheaper house in the trade.
Love-philtre—we've quantities of it;
   And for knowledge if any one burns,

We keep an extremely small prophet, a prophet
   Who brings us unbounded returns:

      For he can prophesy
      With a wink of his eye,
      Peep with security
      Into futurity,
      Sum up your history,
      Clear up a mystery,
      Humour proclivity
      For a nativity—for a nativity;
      With mirrors so magical,
      Tetrapods tragical,
      Bogies spectacular,
      Answers oracular,
      Facts astronomical,
      Solemn or comical,
      And, if you want it, he
      Makes a reduction on taking a quantity!

Oh! if any one anything lacks,
He'll find it all ready in stacks,
    If he'll only look in
    On the resident Djinn,
  Number seventy, Simmery Axe!

He can raise you hosts
      Of Ghosts,
And that without reflectors;
  And creepy things
      With wings,
And gaunt and grisly spectres.
  He can fill you crowds
      Of shrouds,

And horrify you vastly;
   He can rack your brains
      With chains,
And gibberings grim and ghastly!

   Then, if you plan it, he
   Changes organity,
   With an urbanity,
   Full of Satanity,
   Vexes humanity
   With an inanity
   Fatal to vanity—
Driving your foes to the verge of insanity!

   Barring tautology,
   In demonology,
   'Lectro-biology,
   Mystic nosology,
   Spirit philology,
   High-class astrology,
   Such is his knowledge, he
Isn't the man to require an apology!

Oh! my name is John Wellington Wells,
I'm a dealer in magic and spells,
   In blessings and curses
   And ever-filled purses,
In prophecies, witches, and knells.

If any one anything lacks,
He'll find it all ready in stacks,
   If he'll only look in
   On the resident Djinn,
Number seventy, Simmery Axe!

—W. S. GILBERT
The Sorcerer

EXERCISE 15

Songs for Mouth, Lips, and Tongue

Singing requires vigorous lip and tongue action, as well as a proper use of the diaphragm. When you sing, sing both with full gusto and clear articulation. Remember to hold consonants that you might slur or drop in speech. Support final consonants by prolonging them.

As a group exercise, a good routine would be: (1) relaxation exercises, (2) lip and tongue exercises, and (3) the song exercise. Remember that the mouth is a megaphone and must be wide open in order that the voice as an instrument can work properly.

If books are to be held while you sing, please hold them at eye level and not at waist level. Holding a book at eye level will prevent the pressing of the chin into the larynx, the depressing of the vocal cords, and the cutting down of the efficiency of the mouth as a megaphone.

For singing in unison, the lyrics of several familiar songs are provided.

JINGLE BELLS

a.

1. Dashing through the snow, in a one-horse open
       sleigh,
   O'er the fields we go, laughing all the way!
   Bells on bobtail ring, making spirits bright;
   What fun it is to ride and sing a sleighing song
       tonight!

   (*Chorus*)

   Jingle Bells! Jingle Bells! Jingle all the way!
   Oh what fun it is to ride in a one-horse open
       sleigh! (repeat)

2. A day or two ago, I thought I'd take a ride,
   And soon Miss Fannie Bright was seated by my
       side.

The horse was lean and lank; misfortune seemed
    his lot;
He got into a drifted bank, and we, we got upsot.
        (*Chorus*)

3. Now the ground is white; go it while you're
    young;
   Take the girls tonight, and sing this sleighing
    song.
   Just get a bob-tailed bay, two forty for his speed;
   Then hitch him to an open sleigh, and crack,
    you'll take the lead!
        (*Chorus*)

ON TOP OF OLD SMOKY

b.
1. On top of Old Smoky, all covered with snow,
   I lost my true lover by a courtin' too slow.

2. Now courting is pleasure, and parting is grief,
   And a false-hearted true love is worse than a thief.

3. A thief he will rob you, and take what you have,
   But a false-hearted lover will lead you to your
    grave.

4. The grave will decay you and turn you to dust,
   Not one boy in a hundred a poor girl can trust.

5. They'll hug you and kiss you, and tell you more
    lies
   Than the cross-ties on a railroad, or the stars in
    the sky.

6. So come all you young maidens, and listen to me,
   Never place your affection on a green willow tree.

7. For the leaves they will wither and the roots they
        will die,
    You'll all be forsaken, and never know why.

8. On top of Old Smoky, all covered with snow,
    I lost my true lover, from courting too slow.

DAISY

c.

   Daisy, Daisy, give me your answer, do.
   I'm half crazy, over the love of you!
   It won't be a stylish marriage; I can't afford a
       carriage.
   But you'd look sweet, upon the seat
   Of a bicycle built for two!

AULD LANG SYNE

d.

   Should auld acquaintance be forgot and never
       brought to mind?
   Should auld acquaintance be forgot in days of
       Auld Lang Syne?
   For Auld Lang Syne, my dear, for Auld Lang
       Syne,
   We'll take a cup of kindness yet, for Auld Lang
       Syne!

GO DOWN, MOSES

e.
1. When Israel was in Egypt Land (Let my people
       go!)

Oppressed so hard they could not stand (Let my
people go!)
(Chorus)

Go down, Moses, way down in Egypt Land,
Tell old Pharaoh, let my people go!

2. When Israel stood by the water side (Let my
people go!)
At the command of God it did divide (Let my
people go!)
(Chorus)

SHE'LL BE COMIN' ROUND THE MOUNTAIN

f.
1. She'll be comin' around the mountain when she
comes,
She'll be comin' around the mountain when she
comes,
She'll be comin' around the mountain,
She'll be comin' around the mountain,
She'll be comin' around the mountain when she
comes.

2. She'll be drivin' six white horses when she comes,
(repeat)

3. And we'll all go out to meet her when she comes,
(repeat)

4. We'll shout glory hallelujah when she comes,
(repeat)

HE'S GOT THE WHOLE WORLD
IN HIS HANDS

g.
1. He's got the whole world in his hands,
   He's got the whole world in his hands,
   He's got the whole world, in his hands,
   He's got the whole world in his hands!

2. He's got the little babies in his hands, (repeat)
3. He's got the gambling man in his hands, (repeat)
4. He's got you and me, sister, in his hands, (repeat)
5. He's got the whole world in his hands, (repeat)

MY DARLING CLEMENTINE

h.
1. In a cavern, in a canyon, excavating for a mine,
   Dwelt a miner forty-niner, and his daughter,
   Clementine.
   (Chorus)

   Oh my darling, oh my darling, oh my darling
   Clementine!
   You are lost and gone forever, dreadful sorry,
   Clementine!
2. Light she was, and like a fairy, and her shoes were
   number nine;
   Herring boxes without topses, sandals were for
   Clementine.
   (Chorus)

3. Drove she ducklings to the water, every morning
   just at nine,
   Hit her foot against a splinter, fell into the foam-
   ing brine.
   (Chorus)

OLD MCDONALD HAD A FARM

i.
1. Old McDonald had a farm, e, i, e, i, o.
    And on this farm he had some chicks, e, i, e, i, o.
    With a chick chick here, and a chick chick there,
    Here a chick, there a chick, everywhere a chick
        chick,
    Old McDonald had a farm, e, i, e, i, o.
2. Repeat, substituting pigs: oink, oink (repeat
        chicks)
3. Repeat, substituting ducks: quack, quack (repeat
        chicks, pigs)
4. Repeat, substituting cows: moo, moo (repeat
        chicks, pigs, ducks)

YANKEE DOODLE

j.
1. Yankee Doodle went to town, riding on a pony,
    Stuck a feather in his cap, and called it macaroni!
            (*Chorus*)

    Yankee Doodle, keep it up, Yankee Doodle
        Dandy,
    Mind the music and the step, and with the girls
        be handy.

2. Father and I went down to camp, along with
        Captain Goodin,
    And there we saw the men and boys as thick as
        hasty puddin'.
            (*Chorus*)

3. And there was Captain Washington upon a strap-
        ping stallion,

A-giving orders to his men, I guess there was a
million.
>(*Chorus*)

4. And there we saw a thousand men, as rich as
Squire David,
And what they wasted every day, I wish it could
be saved.
>(*Chorus*)

HOME ON THE RANGE

k.
1. O give me a home, where the buffalo roam,
Where the deer and the antelope play,
Where seldom is heard a discouraging word,
And the skies are not cloudy all day.
>(*Chorus*)

Home, home on the range, where the deer and
the antelope play,
Where seldom is heard a discouraging word, and
the skies are not cloudy all day.

2. Where the air is so pure, the zephyrs so free,
The breezes so balmy and bright,
That I would not exchange my home on the
range
For all of the cities so bright.
>(*Chorus*)

3. Oh, give me a land where the bright diamond
sand
Flows leisurely down to the stream;
Where the graceful white swan goes gliding along,
Like a maid in a heavenly dream.
>(*Chorus*)

GIVE ME THAT OLD TIME RELIGION

l.

1.   Give me that old time religion, give me that old
time religion,
Give me that old time religion, it's good enough
for me!

2.   It was good for the Hebrew children, it was good
for the Hebrew children,
It was good for the Hebrew children, and it's
good enough for me!

3.   It was good for Paul and Aaron, it was good for
Paul and Aaron,
It was good for Paul and Aaron, so it's good
enough for me!

4.   It'll be good when the world's on fire, it'll be
good when the world's on fire,
It'll be good when the world's on fire, so it's good
enough for me!

SWING LOW, SWEET CHARIOT

m.

(Chorus)
Swing low, sweet chariot, coming for to carry me
home!
Swing low, sweet chariot, coming for to carry me
home!

1.   I looked over Jordan, and what did I see, coming
for to carry me home?
A band of angels, coming after me, coming for to
carry me home.
(Chorus)

2. If you get there before I do, coming for to carry
   me home,
   Tell all my friends I'm coming too, coming for
   to carry me home.

   (*Chorus*)

3. I'm sometimes up and sometimes down, coming
   for to carry me home,
   But still my soul feels heavenly bound, coming for
   to carry me home.

   (*Chorus*)

AMERICA

1. My country tis of thee, sweet land of liberty,
   Of thee I sing: Land where my fathers died,
   Land of the pilgrim's pride; from every moun-
   tain side,
   Let freedom ring!

2. My native country, thee,
   Land of the noble free,
   Thy name I love:
   I love thy rocks and rills,
   Thy woods and templed hills;
   My heart with rapture thrills,
   Like that above.

CAMPTOWN RACES

o.
1. The Camptown ladies sing this song! Doodah!
   Doodah!
   The Camptown racetrack is nine miles long! Oh
   doodah day!

(*Chorus*)
Going to run all night, going to run all day,
I'll bet my money on the bob-tail nag,
Somebody bet on the bay.

2. I came down with my hat caved in, Doodah!
   Doodah!
   I'll go back with a pocketful of tin! Oh Doodah
   day!

(*Chorus*)

LOCH LOMOND

p.

By yon bonnie banks, and by yon bonnie braes,
Where the sun shines bright on Loch Lomond,
Where me and my true love were ever wont to go,
On the bonnie, bonnie banks of Loch Lomond!
Oh, ye'll take the high road, and I'll take the low
   road,
And I'll be in Scotland afore ye!
But me and my true love will never meet again,
On the bonnie, bonnie banks of Loch Lomond.

GOOD NIGHT LADIES

q.
1. Good night, ladies; good night, ladies;
   Good night, ladies; we're going to leave you now.
        (*Chorus*)

   Merrily we roll along, roll along, roll along,
   Merrily we roll along, o'er the deep blue sea.
2. Sweet dreams, ladies; sweet dreams, ladies;
   Sweet dreams, ladies; we're going to leave you
        now.
        (*Chorus*)

4

Your Speech Profile

*B*efore you start work on the specific sounds of the International Phonetic Alphabet, it will be very useful if your instructor will help you to chart your own, personal *speech profile*, which will act as a dictional guide for this course.

The sentences to follow contain all of the sounds of the IPA. As you read, your instructor will check off those sounds that are problems for you. Then during the semester you should concentrate on those sounds.

Make an important psychological adjustment before you read: namely, resolve to keep in mind that this is not a test to place you in a class rank. As a matter of fact, you should never consider yourself in competition with anyone else in the class. The evaluation is given so that you can compete with yourself. Your grade should depend on how well *you* improve *your own* speech.

You are the core of this course; in fact, you *are* the course. You and your instructor will concentrate on your diction. Take advantage of this opportunity to improve yourself. Working from the speech profile, your instructor will let you know, as the semester proceeds, how you are progressing.

Use the following reading exercises to prepare your speech profile. Your instructor will fill in the evaluation blanks on the Speech Profile chart.

Speech Profile Evaluations

Student's name _____

Class _____

Major subject (or current job) _____

Diction

Consonants needing
  improvement   ____ ____ ____ ____ ____ ____

Vowels needing
  improvement   ____ ____ ____ ____ ____ ____

Pronunciation Errors

Omissions   ____ ____ ____ ____ ____ ____ ____

Additions   ____ ____ ____ ____ ____ ____ ____

Substitutions ____ ____ ____ ____ ____ ____ ____

Vocal Quality

Hoarseness _____

Nasality _____

Inaudibility _____

Other _____

Variety in Speech

Pitch (monotone) _____

Rate   too fast _____

        too slow _____

Volume _____

Pauses _____

Reading for Diction: Vowels

PHONETIC SYMBOL	DIACRITIC SYMBOL	
[i]	ē	Take your seat and greet the speech teacher.
[ɪ]	ĭ	This inventory is invalid if not used as an aid to instruction.
[e]	ā	The pace of the ace was hard to face.
[ɛ]	ĕ	Edna is not wedded or indebted because she fled.
[æ]	ă	The telegram on the program was a sham and that was why he had to dash over the grass with the plaid stamps.
[ɝ]	ûr	He never heard a word, only the song of the bird.
[ɚ]	ẽr	To sever forever, never ever to meet is clever.
[ʌ]	ŭ	She cut the butt, not the cigar butt, but the ham butt, for the mutt.
[ə]	ŭ	All alone in the arena, he looked above, around, and about.
[u]	o͞o	She fluted to the new moon and it loosened its blueness.
[ʊ]	o͝o	He shook in the nook near the brook.
[o]	ō	I'll omit the note, but I'll protest tomorrow to the police.
[ɔ]	ô	It's awful but he's not nautical and is in awe of the water.
[ɑ]	ä	The father is not in the lot with the hot pot.
[eɪ]	ā	(same sound or phoneme as [e]).
[ɑɪ]	ī	Splice the ice and spice it nicely.
[ɔɪ]	oi	He toiled over the spoiled doily for it was oily.
[ɑʊ]	ou	She was loud and proud never to be bowed by a crowd.
[oʊ]	ō	(same sound or phoneme as [o]).

Reading for Diction: Consonants

PHONETIC SYMBOL	DIACRITIC SYMBOL	
[b]	b	Brambles of blueberries burn in beautiful, bright blazes.
[p]	p	Petting pets in parks is prohibited; perhaps it is permitted in parlors.
[d]	d	Dutiful drummers delight in discerning dramatic decibels.
[t]	t	Titivating Titania taunted the tattooed Tartar into a tragic trauma.
[g]	g	Guttenberg gets gyrating geniis to giggle in ghostly ghettoes.
[k]	k	Kukla kicked the camera into kingdom come knocking Kubla Khan cold.
[m]	m	Myriads of mummies mumbled muffled moans into multicolored masks.
[n]	n	Neat Nancy nibbled on the nasty but nourishing noodles and nuts.
[ŋ]	ng	The throng hung onto the singer who was flung back in anger.
[v]	v	Vitamins and vinegar in vast volumes vary in vim and vigor.
[f]	f	Futuristic furniture is fine for fun-finding, frolicking, fancy-free families.
[ð]	t̶h̶	The heathens without clothes writhed to the smooth, seething rhythm.
[θ]	th	Thoreau thought thrillingly about theoretical and thematic Thermopylaes.
[z]	z	A Zuider Zee zoo zoologist said, "Zooie!" to the zebra from Zambezi.
[s]	s	Sussex suspected Susa whose susceptibility seemed seriously suspicious.
[ʒ]	zh	Pleasure is a division of leisure with a measure of vision.

[ʃ]	sh	Shrill shrimpers shouted at the shallow, sharp, shell shippers.
[h]	h	Hieronymus' hell houses hermaphroditic hellhounds and harrowing Hecates.
[l]	l	"Love me, or leave me!" is likely to lump loads of leftover lovers.
[r]	r	A rerun at the Regency ran Ronald Reagan and Rudolph the Red-nosed Reindeer.
[w]	w	Worldly workwomen want wondrous works and won't wed witless wooers.
[ʍ]	hw	Whistler whistled while the whippoorwill whished into the whiffletree.
[j]	y	The young Yahoos yelped, yearned, and yelled for youths in Yokohama.
[dʒ]	j	Juliet jostled the juvenile jury with the jaundiced and the jobless.
[tʃ]	ch	Chicanery in chinchillas and chimpanzees is chock-full of chivalry.

Reading for Rate, Clarity, and Quality

An average rate for clarity in reading the selection below would be in the 120 to 150 words per minute range. This could fall slightly to either side, depending on the interpretation of the reader. Remember that rate in itself is completely flexible, affected not only by the personality of the speaker but also the occasion of the speech. The professional delivery of the race track announcer would be out of place during a funeral eulogy. An ardent suitor, proposing, does not speak at the same rate as an angry husband in an argument.

CRIME AND CRIMINALS
The warden of the Cook County Jail in Chicago, who knew Clarence Darrow as a criminologist, lawyer, and writer, invited

*him to speak before the inmates of the jail. Darrow accepted
the invitation. This was in 1902.*

*The prisoners marched into the auditorium where they
heard what is today still considered one of the most extraordinary
speeches ever delivered to such an audience.*

I will guarantee to take from this jail, or any (10) jail in the
world, five hundred men who have been (20) the worst criminals
and lawbreakers who ever got into jail, (30) and I will go down to
our lowest streets and (40) take five hundred of the most aban-
doned prostitutes, and go (50) out somewhere where there is plenty
of land, and will (60) give them a chance to make a living, and
they (70) will be as good people as the average in the (80) com-
munity.

There is a remedy for the sort of condition (90) we see here. The
world never finds it out, or (100) when it does find it out it does not
enforce (110) it. You may pass a law punishing every person with
(120) death for burglary, and it will make no difference. (130)
Men will commit it just the same. In England there (140) was a
time when one hundred different offenses were punishable (150)
with death, and it made no difference. The English people (160)
strangely found out that so fast as they repealed the (170) severe
penalties and so fast as they did away with (180) punishing men
by death, crime decreased instead of increased; that (190) the
smaller the penalty the fewer the crimes.

Hanging men (200) in our county jails does not prevent murder.
It makes (210) murderers.

And this has been the history of the world. (220) It's easy to see
how to do away with what (230) we call crime. It is not so easy to
do (240) it. I will tell you how to do it. It (250) can be done by
giving the people a chance to (260) live—by destroying special
privileges. So long as big criminals (270) can get the coal fields, so
long as the big (280) criminals have control of the city council
and get (290) the public streets for streetcars and gas rights—this
is (300) bound to send thousands of poor people to jail. So (310)
long as men are allowed to monopolize all the earth, (320) and
compel others to live on such terms as these (330) men see fit to
make, then you are bound to (340) get into jail.

The only way in the world to (350) abolish crime and criminals is to abolish the big ones (360) and the little ones together. Make fair conditions of life. (370) Give men a chance to live. Abolish the right of (380) private ownership of land, abolish monopoly, make the world partners (390) in production, partners in the good things of life. Nobody (400) would steal if he could get something of his own (410) some easier way. Nobody will commit burglary when he has (420) a house full. No girl will go out on the (430) streets when she has a comfortable place at home. The (440) man who owns a sweatshop or a department store may (450) not be to blame himself for the condition of his (460) girls, but when he pays them five dollars, three dollars, (470) and two dollars a week, I wonder where he thinks (480) they will get the rest of their money to live. (490) The only way to cure these conditions is by equality. (500) There should be no jails. They do not accomplish what (510) they pretend to accomplish. If you would wipe them out (520) there would be no more criminals than now. They terrorize (530) nobody. They are a blot upon any civilization, and a (540) jail is an evidence of the lack of charity of (550) the people on the outside who make the jails and (560) fill them with the victims of their greed.

5

Introduction to the International Phonetic Alphabet

The symbols of the IPA, Chart 5-1, can be compared to the notes that you must learn in order to play your musical instrument. You will be a better speaker if you learn the notes by heart, with the proper positioning for each of your articulators: the mouth or jaw, lips, and tongue. A good musician knows not only his notes but also the proper fingering to produce them. If you have worked hard on the preceding chapters, you should be on your way to possession of a relaxed instrument, and you should have articulators that are alive and responsive to commands.

The sounds (or, technically, phonemes) of our language fall broadly into two main groups which you have known since the first or second grade. A *vowel* can be described as a voiced sound that is relatively uninterrupted by the articulators. A *consonant* is a sound that is more modified by the articulators— by the shaping of the lips and tongue, by the touching of the lips or tongue to the teeth, or by the tongue to the gum ridge or to the hard palate. The voiced consonants, like all the vowels, result from an airstream passing from the lungs over the vibrating

66

vocal cords and thence to the moderation by the articulators, which distinguishes them. There are some unvoiced consonants in the production of which the vocal cords do not vibrate.

Types of Vowels and Consonant Sounds

For the purposes of our speech work, we must further divide the vowel and consonant families.

A *diphthong*, in the vowel family, is a combination of two vowel sounds which join to form a single sound. The vowel sound in *sound* is a diphthong, combining the sounds "ah" and "ooh."

Among consonants, a *plosive* is an explosion of air that has been blocked momentarily either by the lips, as in [p] or [b]; by the tongue on the gum ridge, as in [t] or [d]; or by the tongue on the soft palate, as in [k] or [g].

A *nasal* is a consonant made either with the lips or the back of the throat closed so that the vibration must pass through the nasal passages, as in [m], [n], or [ŋ].

Fricatives are consonant sounds in which the air is not completely blocked, but is restricted so that vocal friction results: [f], [v], [ʌ], [θ–ð], [s–z], [ʃ–ʒ], [h].

A *semivowel*, of which there are only two, is a consonant sound that is even less restricted than the fricatives, so that more air escapes, resulting in a sound not unlike a vowel sound. The semivowels are [l] and [r].

Notice how we have proceeded from the plosive and the nasal which result from complete air blockage, to the fricative which results from semiblockage, and finally to the semivowel which results from almost no blockage. The vowel and the diphthong, then, result from the least blockage of all.

Other Sounds

Besides these subdivisions of the vowel and consonant families, there are two other kinds of sounds: the *glide* and the *combination plosive-fricative* sound. The glide is made with an

CHART 5-1. The International Phonetic Alphabet (IPA)

CONSONANTS

IPA SYMBOL	SAMPLE	DESCRIPTION
[b]	boy	voiced plosive
[p]	pull	unvoiced plosive
[d]	do	voiced plosive
[t]	to	unvoiced plosive
[g]	go	voiced plosive
[k]	car	unvoiced plosive
[m]	main	voiced nasal
[n]	now	voiced nasal
[ŋ]	sing	voiced nasal
[v]	very	voiced fricative
[f]	full	unvoiced fricative
[ð]	that	voiced fricative
[θ]	think	unvoiced fricative
[z]	zoom	voiced fricative
[s]	sea	unvoiced fricative
[ʒ]	measure	voiced fricative
[ʃ]	shell	unvoiced fricative
[h]	how	unvoiced fricative
[l]	love	voiced semivowel
[r]	rub	voiced semivowel
[w]	will	voiced glide
[ʍ]	where	unvoiced glide
[j]	young	voiced glide
[dʒ]	just	voiced combination plosive-fricative
[tʃ]	chin	unvoiced combination plosive-fricative

VOWELS

[i]	eat	frontal vowel
[ɪ]	it	frontal vowel
[e]	locate	frontal vowel unstressed syllable

CHART 5-1. The International Phonetic Alphabet (IPA), cont'd

VOWELS (CONT'D)

IPA SYMBOL	SAMPLE	DESCRIPTION
[ɛ]	m*e*t	frontal vowel
[æ]	s*a*t	frontal vowel
[a]†	h*a*lf	frontal vowel
[ɝ]	b*ir*d	medial vowel, stressed syllable
[ɚ]	ev*er*	medial vowel, unstressed syllable
[ʌ]	c*u*t	medial vowel, stressed syllable
[ə]	*a*bove	medial vowel, unstressed syllable
[u]	m*oo*n	back vowel
[ʊ]	t*oo*k	back vowel
[o]*	*o*bey	back vowel
[ɔ]	*a*we	back vowel
[ɒ]†	h*o*t	back vowel
[ɑ]	f*a*ther	back vowel

DIPHTHONGS

[eɪ]*	*a*ce	diphthong
[aɪ]	*i*ce	diphthong
[ɔɪ]	*oi*l	diphthong
[aʊ]	c*ow*	diphthong
[oʊ]*	fl*oa*t	diphthong

NOTE: * Phoneticians now virtually agree that the sound of the phoneme [e] can scarcely be differentiated from the sound of the diphthong [eɪ], and that the sound of the phoneme [o] can scarcely be differentiated from the sound of the diphthong [oʊ]. It is now acceptable to use the phonemes [e] and [o] in all instances.

† These sounds are found in eastern New England speech and seldom occur in General American Speech.

articulator in motion; [w] and [j] are the two glide sounds of the IPA. The combination plosive-fricative sound can be illustrated by the [tʃ] of church, where the tongue makes a slight [t] before going on to the [ʃ] sound. The same phenomenon happens when the word *judge* is pronounced, combining in the initial letter the sounds [d] and [ʒ].

In the various sound-charts in this chapter, the word *voiced* indicates simply a sound in which the vocal cords are vibrating. In an unvoiced sound as the [θ] in *bath*, the vocal cords do not vibrate. For a simple test when you are in doubt about the distinction, put your hand on your throat and slowly make the sound. You will know by the presence or absence of vibration whether the sound is voiced or unvoiced.

There are forty-four sounds in the IPA and only twenty-six letters in the English language. This is why our language is so difficult to spell, and distinctions are so hard to make. What about *book* and *boot, shook* and *shoot?* Spelled phonetically [bʊk, but; ʃʊk, ʃut] these words would be self-explanatory to grammar-school child and foreign student alike. George Bernard Shaw was so dedicated to the dream of phonetically-spelled English that he left a part of his estate to further the cause. If English were spelled phonetically, we would have no problems like that of the foreign student who came to me trained by his English teacher to pronounce [s] as [z] in the important words *his, was, is, has, does,* and so on. I had the task of persuading him that *this* and *miss* were not pronounced *thizz* and *mizz*.

IPA CONSONANTS

Of the twenty-five consonants in the IPA, Chart 5-2, only nine do not appear in the English alphabet. They are [ŋ], [θ], [ð], [ʃ], [ʒ], [ʍ], [j], [dʒ], [tʃ]. The remaining sixteen symbols or letters are from the English alphabet. Let us briefly examine these nine variant IPA symbols to discover what sounds they represent.

CHART 5-2. IPA Consonants

		Description	Two Lips	Lip-Teeth	Tongue-Teeth	Tongue-Gum Ridge	Tongue-Hard Palate	Tongue-Soft Palate	Vocal Cords
Plosives	voiced	an explosion following a total blockage of air by lips or tongue	b			d		g	
Plosives	voiceless		p			t		k	
Nasals	voiced	lips closed / tongue blocking mouth opening / back of throat closed	m			n		ŋ	
Fricatives	voiced	partial blockage of air		v	ð	z	ʒ		
Fricatives	voiceless			f	θ	s	ʃ		h
Semivowels	voiced	less air blockage than fricatives				l	r		
Glides	voiced	lips in motion throughout	w				j		
Glides	voiceless		ʍ						
Combinations	voiced						dʒ		
Combinations	voiceless						tʃ		

The glide [ŋ], as in *ring, sing, thing,* is made by lowering the velum and raising the back of the tongue to make firm contact so that air is directed through the nose. This is why [ŋ] is classified as a nasal sound. Historically, [ŋg] was used when the

[g] was pronounced. It can still be heard in such words as *stronger* or *strongest*, *young* or *youngest*, and in other comparative or superlative adjectives. For our purposes, let us agree that there is little variation between [ŋ] and [ŋg] when the [g] is dropped in modern usage.

[θ] and [ð] are symbols of the unvoiced and voiced *th*. Unvoiced you remember, simply means that the vocal cords do not vibrate. The unvoiced [θ] is found in words like *think, bath,* and *wrath*. The voiced [ð] is found in words like *that, other,* and *bother*. Both the voiced and the unvoiced *th* require the same tongue placement. The tip of the tongue should be placed lightly between the teeth in order to avoid the [t] or [d] that would result if the tip of the tongue were to touch the gum ridge —producing *dis* for *this*, or *tink* for *think*.

[ʃ], and [ʒ] are paired because they too are unvoiced and voiced phonemes that require the same lip and tongue placement. [ʃ] occurs in *fish, dish, she, ship,* and *hash* and in *motion, nation, remission, machine*. To distinguish the [ʃ], first sound an *s* as if you were hissing (not the [ʃ]); then, for the[ʃ], *sh* as if you were trying to silence someone. There is a noticeable difference in the tension of the tongue. An [s] requires a tense and narrow tongue arched against the gum ridge, causing air to flow in a thin stream. The [ʃ] requires a tongue pulled slightly back and flattened out, causing air to flow in a broader, heavier stream.

[ʒ] is made just as is the unvoiced [ʃ] except that the vocal cords vibrate. [ʒ] is found in words like *pleasure, azure,* or *vision*.

[ʍ] is the unvoiced counterpart of [w]. It is interesting to note that in Old English, the words *when* and *where* were spelled *hwen* and *hwere*. To this day that influence is still heard in [ʍ] words like *what, when, where,* and *why*. [w] is voiced, as in *we, wail, watt, wet* and *wine*.

The glide [j] is the first sound in *yet*, or *yes*. [j] is voiced and in words like *union, unity, student,* and *you* it is combined with the vowel sound *u* as in *moon*, phonetically [u]. Phonetically, [ju] is *you*.

[tʃ] and [dʒ] are paired because they share the same lip and tongue placement as do [t] and [d]. [t] is a voiceless plosive and its sounded counterpart is [d]. Place your fingers lightly on your throat and pronounce the word *church*. Now pronounce the word *judge*. *Church* contains the sound [tʃ] twice and is voiceless, whereas the word *judge* contains the sound [dʒ] twice and is voiced. The combinations of the consonant *t* with the [ʃ] and the consonant *d* with [ʒ] occur so quickly that it is almost impossible to separate them. We shall encounter this phenomenon again when we study diphthongs, which are combinations of two joined vowel sounds.

The remaining IPA symbols for consonants are all identical with the letters of the alphabet, but it must be clearly understood that the sounds of the IPA and the sounds of the letters of the alphabet are not the same thing. For example, if you were to pronounce the letters of the alphabet you would say *pee* for the letter *p*, or *zee* for the letter *z*, each time adding the vowel sound *eee* [i] in a consonant-vowel combination that has nothing to do with the exact sound of a phonetically sounded [p] or [z]. In our spoken language, [p] is only a puff of air, accurately classified as voiceless plosive consonant. [z] is a voiced fricative that sounds like a buzzing *zzzz*.

IPA VOWELS

The International Phonetic Alphabet gives an accurate system of sound notation. Now you must learn to produce the required sound with accuracy. When we discussed certain consonant sounds, you were asked to get the *feeling* of the sound in your mouth. This is an important point and can't be over-emphasized. The "ear" alone cannot be trusted to help produce the desired sound, especially in the case of vowels which are more flowing than consonants and therefore are more difficult to control. So if you will concentrate on the feeling of your tongue and lips when you shape a vowel sound, you will avoid the difficulties experienced by the following students.

One student could not properly sound the vowel in *law* without using an intrusive *r*; he consistently said *lore*. His ear told him he was saying *law*, but he always said *lore*. Another student could not pronounce the word *back*. He would say *beck*. No matter how many times I insisted upon *back*, invariably, each time he persisted in answering *beck!* with great conviction.

A Spanish-speaking student confused the [i] and [ɪ] sounds as found in the words *eat* and *it*. He would always say *eat* for *it* as, "Eat is a hot day!" Conversely, he would substitute *it* for *eat*, saying "*It* the bread!"

In each instance these students thought they were accurately producing the correct sounds because their ears deceived them and they never showed any improvement until they got the *feeling* of the sounds in their tongues and their lips. This, I believe, proves the unreliability of the ear alone and the futility of the mimicry or parrot method of teaching speech. Learn the correct placement of your articulators for each sound.

IPA EXERCISES

Included among the exercises in the next six chapters are several that require you to look up the diacritical markings that denote certain words. The diacritical marks used in dictionaries are those dashes, curves, dots, quotation marks, and other markings placed over letters to help our alphabet do what it cannot do on its own: represent all the sounds of the English language. Unfortunately, each dictionary uses a method of its own, and there will be differences. To avoid arguments, the class should agree to use a standard dictionary. Paperback dictionaries are not adequate for the exercises that follow. Every college student should possess a good hard covered desk dictionary. The price, pro-rated over a four year period, makes this a very good buy. The following hard covered dictionaries are recommended for use on all the vocabulary drills that follow:

Webster's Eighth Collegiate Dictionary
  (Merriam Webster Co.)
Webster's New World Dictionary
  (Collins-World Publishing Co.)
American Heritage Dictionary
  (Houghton Mifflin Co.)
Random House College Dictionary
  (Random House)

We are now going to take each of the forty-four phonetic symbols in turn and learn to make their sounds properly. You will find that most of these forty-four sounds are not troublesome to you, but it will help your speech to know just how they are made. When you find a sound that *is* troublesome to you, spend more time on it.

We shall take consonants first. You will never achieve clarity in speaking English without good, firm consonants. English can be imagined as a stream of water across which is a bridge of stepping stones. The vowels are the flowing water, the consonants the stones upon which you must step firmly and from which you must not slip. Furthermore, correct enunciation of consonants will help you to overcome too-rapid speech and mumbling.

6

IPA Consonants:
Plosives and Nasals

he IPA consonant *plosives* are sounds produced by an explosion following a momentary blockage of air by the lips or tongue. IPA consonant nasals, you will remember, are produced by vibration passing through nasal passages, with either lips or back of the throat closed.

PLOSIVES

There are two basic types of plosives: *voiced* and *voiceless*. *Voiced* plosives include the letters b, d, and g. *Voiceless* plosives include the letters *p*, *t*, and *k*. In the first part of Chapter Six (and in Exercise 16), we shall study the voiced plosive [*b*] and the voiceless plosive [*p*]. Later, with Exercise 17, we shall study the voiced plosive [*d*] and the voiceless plosive [*t*]. Finally, Exercise 18 will allow us to review the voiced plosive [g] and the voiceless plosive [k].

CHART 6-1. The IPA Consonant Plosives [b] and [p].

IPA Symbol	Sample	Type	Tongue	Lips or Mouth	Vocal Cords
b	boy	voiced plosive	neutral	closed tightly until explosive release of air	vibrating
p	pull	unvoiced plosive			non-vibrating

Note that the pairs of sounds in the plosive family always have the same lip, mouth, and tongue positions. They differ only in being voiced or voiceless. In step one of Exercises 16 and 17, place your fingers on your neck where you can feel your vocal cords. You will discover that the difference between the two sounds is only that on one the vocal cords vibrate and on the other they do not.

EXERCISE 16

[b] and [p] Sounds
See Chart 6-1

1. Recite each horizontal and vertical group three times. Open your mouth as widely as possible on the "ah" sounds. Remember that in exercise work you exaggerate:

[b]ah	[b]ah	[b]ah	[b]ah
[p]ah	[p]ah	[p]ah	[p]ah
[b]ah	[b]ah	[b]ah	[b]ah
[p]ah	[p]ah	[p]ah	[p]ah

2. Pronounce the following words containing [b]. Be careful not to stress final plosives:

Initial	Medial	Final
boot	rubber	hub
bib	rabbit	blab
bet	mobster	nib
bat	Webster	web
boom	tuber	blub
barn	blubber	blob

3. Pronounce the following words containing [p]:

Initial	Medial	Final
peach	soporific	trap
push	propagate	lip
posh	nippers	warp
pest	malpractice	vamp
plum	lumpish	trump
pack	happiness	skimp

4. To feel the distinction between [p] and [b], read aloud the following pairs of words:

bitter pickle	piebald biped
pitiful brigand	perfect balderdash
powerful blunderbuss	beautiful Penelope
Brobdingnagian people	Pandora's box
proper bombast	blooming pansy
platitudinous jabber	purple bagpipe
boiling Pablum	peppy bumblebee
pesky boy	Beppo's pub

5. The words below are not properly matched. Pronounce each word in the left-hand column; then write its number next to its phonetic counterpart. The purpose of the exer-

cise is twofold: you will pronounce the sounds you are
studying, and you will get to know their phonetic symbols.

1. bad _____ bɪtʃ
2. best _____ bɪljən
3. bash _____ bæd
4. balloon _____ blɝ
5. bleed _____ blænd
6. billion _____ bɛst
7. bitch _____ bɪskɪt
8. bland _____ bə'lun
9. biscuit _____ bæʃ
10. blur _____ blid

1. path _____ pʌb
2. pet _____ prɪg
3. prince _____ prɪns
4. protest _____ pik
5. pub _____ 'pætɚ
6. prig _____ pæθ
7. penury _____ pɛt
8. peek _____ 'protɛst
9. patter _____ pæʃən
10. passion _____ 'pɛnjəri

6.   Recite as quickly as possible with accuracy:

> The Owl and the Pussy-cat went to sea
> In a beautiful pea-green boat,
> They took some honey, and plenty of money,
> Wrapped up in a five-pound note.
> The Owl looked up to the stars above,
> And sang to a small guitar,
> 'O lovely Pussy! O Pussy, my love,
> What a beautiful Pussy you are,
>   You are,
>   You are!
> What a beautiful Pussy you are!'

—EDWARD LEAR
The Owl and the Pussycat

7.   Look up the following words in your hardcovered dictionary. Next to each word write its diacritical equivalent and
the first definition given. All of these words will be found
in the reading below. If you do not look up the vocabulary
words you don't know, you are only hurting yourself. The
importance of vocabulary building for college students can
not be overemphasized.

	DIACRITICS	DEFINITIONS
brontosaurus		
blithesomely		
Boston Brahmins		
belletrists		
Boyards		
Bedouins		
William Butler Yeats		
bourgeoisie		
bromides		
bodkins		
blunderbusses		
bicuspid		
Beau Brummell		
Brunhild		
Brueghel		
Dante's Beatrice		
Boniface		
Botticelli		
nimbus		
beatified		
Brobdingnagian		
behemoth		
bowdlerized		
borzois		
Bosporus		
bibliomaniacs		
bouillabaisse		

8. Read this the first time slowly for accuracy. Then in subsequent readings, try for interpretation and expression.

Beneath the biggest Big Dipper a baleful, bashful brontosaurus blithesomely bore on his broad back a bunch of Boston Brahmins, belletrists, who were serving brunch to a batch of boisterous Bolshivikis, a bunch of blue-bearded Boyards, a bedful of Bedouins from Byzantium (ballyhooed by William Butler Yeats), plus a biggish bushel-basket of blundering, bawdy bourgeoisie bearing bottles of bubbly brew, babbling bromides, brandishing bare bodkins, bulldogs, books of braille, Brussels sprouts, Bronx cheers, barbells, blunderbusses, billiard balls, brocolli branches, and bundles of brochures of Boulder Dam, Beverly Hills, and the Land of Beulah! On bronte's tail 'neath the bam, 'neath the boo, 'neath the bamboo tree sat a blob of bicuspid boobies beating on bongo drums; beautiful Beau Brummell, bosomy Brunhild, boastful Bonaparte, brushy Brueghel, Dante's Beatrice, bullish Boniface, beatific Buddha, Venus-bearing Botticelli, and tooth-braced Bogart doing the boogie-woogie with baby-faced Bacall. Meanwhile, our beneficent brontosaurus babbled into a balmy breeze brief bravissimos, as a batch of nimbus shaped butterflies beati-fied the Brobdingnagian behemoth. This block-busting finale has never been rivaled by any Broadway blast or any Beverly Hills bowdlerized, double "B" rated bomb. It will be babbled about by the borzois on the Bosphorus, the buzzards of Buzzards Bay, and blue-nosed bibliomaniacs blowing over bowls of boiling bouillabaisse!

9. Look up the following words in *Webster's New International Dictionary*. Next to each word write its diacritical equivalent and the first definition given. All the words will be found in the reading below.

	DIACRITICS	DEFINITIONS
peripatetic		
Pickwickian		
polygynous		
polyandric		
polychromatic		
pernicious		
plug-ugly		
picadors		
polygraphs		
portmanteaus		
Plutarch		

Pliny   _____   _____
Proust   _____   _____
Pope   _____   _____
Pythagoras   _____   _____
plethora   _____   _____
pulchritudinous   _____   _____
pliant   _____   _____
piquant   _____   _____
potentates   _____   _____
prehensile   _____   _____
piscivorous   _____   _____
poltergeists   _____   _____
penumbra   _____   _____

10. Read this the first time slowly for accuracy. In subsequent readings, try for interpretation and expression.

The Pirates of Penzance paddled their pompom packed peripatetic prairie schooner up Penobscot Bay with such Pickwickian pluck that a pack of polygynous, polyandric and polychromatic periwinkles passionately applauded in puddles of perspiration. In pernicious pursuit came a pot-bellied Pinkerton plus a posse of pooh-poohing, plug-ugly, primping, picadors prattling public praises of their perfectly portable polygraphs. Each pirate packed a puffin, a platy-pus, a porpoise, plus portmanteaus piled with popular port-folios of Plutarch, Pliny, Proust, Pope (Alex, of course), Paul the Apostle, and every penny-wise publisher's passion, Pythagoras! A plethora of pulchritudinous, Polynesian princesses plowed plushy, powerful pelvises in proud, pliant, piquant pirouettes. On the poop deck plastered potentates prowled, plucking pulpy pickles from prehensile, pisciv-orous, poltergeists, who pounded on peppermint podiums while pelting the populace with pounds and pounds of plastic ping-pong pellets. Profoundly preoccupied, a por-trait painter prevented playboys pushing perambulators from parading up Pike's Peak with the protection of profane policemen. His speciality was painting packets of posters displaying parrots, prima donnas, poodles, warped planks plugged with plaster of Paris and parcels of pasta, pumpernickel, pickled herring, pistachio nuts, purple plums, polished Packards, pliers, pure penumbra, peonies, peers, peer groups, pelicans, peacocks, and peanut plants. He avoided painting pearls, pears, and Patagonians!

CHART 6-2. The IPA Consonant Plosives [d] and [t].

IPA Symbol	Sample	Type	Tongue	Lips or Mouth	Vocal Cords
d	*do*	voiced plosive	tip against gum ridge behind upper teeth, sides against upper teeth	neutral	vibrating
t	*to*	unvoiced plosive			non-vibrating

The sounds [d] and [t] are made by placing the tip of the tongue firmly against the gum ridge and the sides of the tongue firmly against the inside of the upper teeth and building up a pocket of air which then explodes into the sound. Beware of using the blade (the broad part) of the tongue on the gum ridge to make your [t]; this will result in a sloppy or splashy [t] with a cymbal-like sound.

EXERCISE 17
[d] and [t] Sounds

1. Exaggerating lip and tongue action, recite each horizontal and vertical group three times:

[d]ah	[d]ah	[d]ah	[d]ah
[t]ah	[t]ah	[t]ah	[t]ah
[d]ah	[d]ah	[d]ah	[d]ah
[t]ah	[t]ah	[t]ah	[t]ah

Listen carefully to your [t]. If it sounds sloppy, or splashes with a cymbal-like sound, go back to the tongue exercises (10 through 13) and do more mirror work to point the tongue.

2. Pronounce the following words containing [d]:

Initial	Medial	Final
darn	admit	mid
dim	wooded	mislead
deem	condone	morbid
drown	brandy	told
doom	hinder	build
dime	bonded	thread

3. Pronounce the following words containing [t]:

Initial	Medial	Final
tune	tentative	brat
tinker	theatrics	zealot
trigonometry	tattler	pert
triune	tautology	literate
tête-à-tête	brittle	conduct
tilt	secretive	nut

4. To feel the distinction between [d] and [t], read aloud the following pairs of words:

deride totally	tasty dish
bold tailor	velvet doily
loud talk	exact demand
doomed terrapin	deepest hinterland
Old Testament	dotted tadpole
total dud	inhibit demons

inspired tramp   tedious deed
tongue-tied date   tempera diptych

5. The words below are not properly matched. Pronounce the
    word in the left-hand column; then write its number next to
    its phonetic counterpart.

1. tutor _____ taŋgo
2. tall _____ 'tælo
3. tax _____ tuθ
4. taproot _____ tɪp
5. tango _____ tutɚ
6. tallow _____ trɑd
7. tooth _____ tætlɚ
8. tip _____ tæprut
9. trod _____ tæks
10. tattler _____ tɔl

1. dig _____ drov
2. dug _____ dɑrt
3. drove _____ drɪft
4. draft _____ dɛd
5. draw _____ drim
6. dead _____ dɪm
7. dream _____ dɪg
8. dim _____ dræft
9. dart _____ dʌg
10. drift _____ drɔ

6. Read aloud, paying close attention to the placement of the
    tip of the tongue:

> Lorenzo dwelt at Heighington,
>   (His coat was made of Dimity,)
> Leastways if not exactly there,
>   Yet in its close proximity.
> He called on me—he stayed to tea—
>   Yet not a word he ut-tered,
> Until I said, 'D'ye like your bread
>   Dry?' and he answered 'Buttered.'
> Noodle dumb
> Has a noddle-head,
> I hate such noodles, *I* do.
>
> —LEWIS CARROLL
> *The Legend of Scotland*
> (spelling modernized)

7. Look up the following words in your hardcovered diction-
    ary. Next to each word write its diacritical equivalent and

the first definition given. All of these words will be found in the reading below.

	Diacritics	Definitions
dog day		
disconsolate		
disheveled		
dexterously		
declaim		
decibels		
doggerel		
deifying		
dirge		
demonic		
dotty		
diatribe		
deletions		
doddering		
deus ex-machina		
diurnal		

8. Read the following slowly for accuracy. In subsequent readings try for interpretation and expression.

Devilish dirty Dick's dingy dirigible descended in a dizzy dive, dividing a dense field of dandelions on a despicable dog day, followed by droves of disconsolate, disheveled, dexterously diving dodo birds. Dick delighted to declaim in dramatic decibels and delivered doggone, dogged, doggerel from the top of a doghouse roof where lived dalmatians, dachshunds, Doberman pinschers, and a doggie named Duty. The doting dodo birds droned devoutly to disconsolate Dick in a deifying dirge. Dethroned Dick, not to disoblige, dispatched a demonic, dotty diatribe.

"Ding bats! dummies! dopes! dunderheads! ding-a-lings! and dung drips!"

The dense dodo birds devoured Deadeye Dick's diatribe. They danced in depraved devotion to their dotty dictator.

"Dippety-doo! Dick we dote on you!"

"Dippity-dus do, do, dote on us too!"

In disgust, Dick dumped down a dizzy dish of documentation on the delirious dodos.

"Duty to deletions, devotion to deletions, determination to deletions!"

Dick dribbled on as a dank, deep, dew-drenched darkness decended on the drove of damp dodos, and Dick developed his diatribe, "Don't deliver data to doddering doglegs! Distrust dictating discs and detecting devices." The dodos all died, drowned to death but devoted to a doghouse divinity.

Displeased, Dick dispatched his deus ex-machina dirigible into the diurnal dusk.

9. Look up the following words in your hardcovered dictionary. Next to each word write its diacritical equivalent and the first definition given. All of these words will be found in the reading below.

	DIACRITICS	DEFINITIONS
turgid		
terpsichorean		
transfigured		
tiddlywinks		
titillate		
tepid		
telepathic		
temerariously		
telesthetic		
tenacious		
temporizations		
tendentious		

terminate   _____   _____
turbulent   _____   _____
trysts   _____   _____

10.   Read the following slowly for accuracy. In subsequent readings try for interpretation and expression.

Little Tommy Tucker, a tireless Timbuctoo trucker and a teasing, tearjerking, turgid terpsichorean, took time to tantalize Tilly-Tu-Tu who was totally togaed, and toiled throbbingly, over tubs of Tommy Tucker's teeming, teamster tears, while troops of tough, tempestuous Trojans taunted Tommy Tucker, the trucker, from the tottering towers of Troy, trippingly with their tattling Trojan tongues.

"Toys, toys, total toys in toyland!" Transfigured Tilly thumpingly ticked off tidal waves of tick-tack-toes and tiddlywinks.

Trite Tommy Tucker, the teamster trucker, thought it time to take a tumble at a tough tongue twister too! He tempted to titillate Tilly-Tu-Tu with this thin, tippsy titter. "Tilly-Tu-Tu, take tit for that! Oh, drat, I meant tat! Take tit for tat!"

Tilly-Tu-Tu on tiptoe twisted, trembled, and trotted out trite, trashy trivialities. " 'Tis true; 'tis true; 'tis pity and pity 'tis, 'tis true!" Tepid Tilly-Tu-Tu, now torrid, trod triumphantly to "Tomorrow, and tomorrow, and tomorrow trips me, tips me into two and twenty? Nay, traitor time ticks to thirty! 'Tis true, 'tis true the trying thirties and, twenties too, are tainted. Out, out tanned spot!"

Telepathic tramps, temerariously telesthetic, tap danced to the tempo of tenacious Tilly's temporizations. Tilly trumpeted.

"Tendentious tramps, trip out, terminate, trooping off to terrible, turbulent trysts as tippling troops for tyrants!"

The tramps, Trojans, and Tommy the trucker teamster thundered thanks on tom-toms to the tinkle of toppling Troy.

CHART 6-3. The IPA Consonant Plosives [g] and [k].

IPA Symbol	Sample	Type	Tongue	Lips or Mouth	Vocal Cords
g	go	voiced plosive	tip of tongue pressed behind bottom front teeth, back of tongue pressed against soft palate until sudden release of air	partially open	vibrating
k	car	unvoiced plosive			non-vibrating

EXERCISE 18

[g] and [k] Sounds

1. Recite each horizontal and vertical group three times:

[g]ah   [g]ah   [g]ah   [g]ah
[k]ah   [k]ah   [k]ah   [k]ah
[g]ah   [g]ah   [g]ah   [g]ah
[k]ah   [k]ah   [k]ah   [k]ah

2. Pronounce the following words containing [g]:

Initial	Medial	Final
giddy	begat	stag
grunt	ingot	leg
greet	finger	rig
gum	forgive	log
good	foggy	gag
gold	hungry	dug

3. Pronounce the following words containing [k]:

Initial	Medial	Final
cool	picture	brisk
cop	likely	took
creep	thinking	broke
kin	recoil	muck
kelp	rector	rock
cull	vicar	take

4. To feel the distinction between [g] and [k], read aloud the following pairs of words:

staggering cat	kicking kangaroo
big stick	leaking gasket
angel cake	exotic cargo
country girl	crisp gherkin
rug rack	muckraking demagogue
wicket gate	black gander
current governor	log cabin
leggy colt	Gold Coast

5. The words below are not properly matched. Pronounce the word in the left-hand column; then write its number next to its phonetic counterpart.

1. goad _____ gɛtˌʌp		1. knife _____ kɪlo	
2. grease _____ gæs		2. knell _____ 'kɛtʃəp	
3. ground _____ dʒin		3. kith _____ krɛmlɪn	
4. gig _____ gɔl		4. kin _____ kɪŋ	
5. getup _____ gæŋ		5. kilo _____ krɪpɚ	
6. gas _____ gʌsto		6. ketchup _____ naɪf	
7. gene _____ graʊnd		7. Kremlin _____ nɛl	
8. gall _____ gɪg		8. king _____ kɪn	
9. gang _____ god		9. kipper _____ ki	
10. gusto _____ gris		10. key _____ kɪθ	

6. Recite as quickly as possible with accuracy:

> Hark, hark, the snark,
> Galumphing through the park!
> No passenger of the Ark,
> Cognition is no lark,
> For a snark has no bark.
> What can it do?
> Like nothing in the zoo
> It grins, it grunts and coos
> And sports its pink tattoos.

7. Look up the following words in your hardcovered diction-
    ary. Next to each word write its diacritical equivalent and
    the first definition given.

	DIACRITICS	DEFINITIONS
galactic		
glissando		
gargoyles		
gyrating		
grottoes		
glacial		
gurus		
Galatea		
Galahad		
gauntlet		
gesticulating		
gnomes		
glockenspiels		
Gilgamesh		
Gargantuan		
Götterdämerung		
Gladstone		
grandiloquently		
Gauguin		

Gandhi
Gregory the Great
gavotted
gazebo

8. Read the following slowly for accuracy. In subsequent readings try for interpretation and expression.

A garlanded, galactic galleon glided in a grand glissando from gaseous galaxies over our glittering globe, as goggled-eyed gawkers gaped, gagged, grunted, groaned, gabbled, and gulped gallons of grog and gnawed gobs of garlic in Galveston, Grenoble, Glastonbury, Genoa, and Glasgow. Others gathered on great walls, golden gates, gleaming gondolas, gruesome gargoyles, Gothic gutters, gyrating garrets, ghostly granite gravestones, and gritty green grottoes.

Down the galleon's glacial gangway groped a glum group of gurus clanging Grecian gongs, followed by a gaggle of geese; then gorgeous girl gymnasts gurgled in gung-ho gusto grand Gregorian chants. Galatea grasping Galahad's gauntlet, gesticulated generously; gloomy gnomes banged on glistening glockenspiels under the guidance of a growling Gilgamesh. Next came golden girdled goddesses giggling and grinning gaily, gripping great gilded gladioluses.

Nearby a group of gypsies greased with goose grease a Gargantuan grinding gramophone which ground out globs of the Götterdämerung. In a grandstand Gladstone grandiloquently granted grand tours to grandmothers with gout. This was greeted gravely by Gauguin, Gandhi, Greta Garbo, and Gregory the Great as they gaily gavotted in a grape-graced gazebo!

9. Look up the following words in your hardcovered dictionary. Next to each word write its diacritical equivalent and the first definition given. All of these words will be found in the reading below.

	DIACRITICS	DEFINITIONS
Caligula		
kleptomaniacs		
Khyber		
cul-de-sac		
Clytemnestra		
Calypso		
cadenza		
Cleopatra		
cockatrice		
Krupps		
calligraphy		
caddishly		
kangaroo court		
kelp		
kosher		
katzenjammer		
kitschy		
koala		
kiwi		

10. Read the following slowly for accuracy. In subsequent readings, try for interpretation and expression.

   Caligula, the crook, called his conspiratorial kleptomaniacs to his cloudless club in a Khyber cul-de-sac. Crawling to his cave came his cockeyed cronies, Clytemnestra, a karate killer, Calypso, a cadenza-crooning canary, Cleopatra, a cockatrice-cuddling conniver, and Clementine, a clumsy, clod-clogger. The Krupps came carrying carbines and copies of the Kaiser's calligraphy. From cabarets in Killarney, Killkenny, Kalamazoo and Kansas, came the Ku Klux Klan and kin, the Knights of Kause Kosta, and clubby Kiwanians, accompanied by kilt-clad, cute Kewpie dolls.
   Cockily cutting a camphor-covered cake, Caligula caddishly kidded his comrades in a cackling kangaroo court. Crows clawed clods of kelp from cans, cluttering the crooks'

camp. A Calcutta cook, kerchief capped, kept clobbering crispy clumps of cabbage. Caligula commanded that he keep a kosher kitchen!

Into this katzenjammer confusion came camels carrying cloven-hoofed clowns cackling crazily, clasping kitschy candles, while a koala cub clinked clumsily at a cozy, corned keyboard, and a kiwi clanged on kettledrums in a quick cadence. The complete kit and caboodle collapsed in a catastrophic climax. Kaput!

NASALS

The *nasals* are sounds that are produced by a vibration passing through the nasal passages with either the lips or throat closed. All three nasals are *voiced* sounds: [m], [n], and [ŋ]. Exercises 19 and 20 review the nasal sounds.

CHART 6-4. The IPA Consonant Nasals [m] and [n].

IPA Symbol	Sample	Type	Tongue	Lips or Mouth	Vocal Cords
m	main	voiced nasal	neutral	closed	vibrating
n	now	voiced nasal	tip pressed against upper gum ridge, sides against inside upper teeth to force air through nose	slightly open	vibrating

EXERCISE 19
[m] *and* [n] *Sounds*

The sounds [m] and [n] are discussed together for purposes of contrast. They are sometimes confused because of poor articulation, and the distinction between them will become clearer when they are studied together.

1. Recite each horizontal and vertical group three times, holding the bracketed sound for four seconds:

[*m*]ah	[*m*]ah	[*m*]ah	[*m*]ah
[*n*]ah	[*n*]ah	[*n*]ah	[*n*]ah
[*m*]ah	[*m*]ah	[*m*]ah	[*m*]ah
[*n*]ah	[*n*]ah	[*n*]ah	[*n*]ah

(You will frequently be asked to hold a sound for four seconds, now that you have passed the plosives, which by their nature cannot be held. A good system for counting while you hold the sound is to tap your four fingers on the table consecutively or to hold up your hand, curling your fingers down consecutively at the rate of one a second.)

2. Slowly pronounce the following words, which contain [m], holding the [m] for four seconds:

Initial	*Medial*	*Final*
motion	rhyming	tomb
maiden	rumble	hymn
music	thimble	room
manly	gamble	lamb
most	booming	blame
mist	chiming	come

3. Slowly pronounce the following words, which contain [n], holding the [n] for four seconds:

Initial	Medial	Final
net	annul	man
nought	annex	plane
neither	nunnery	in
knit	banner	main
nip	finish	on
knack	trundle	moon

4. To feel the distinction between [m] and [n], read aloud the following pairs of words:

moon maiden	numbing Nembutal
bitten mutton	mere nincompoop
numerous enthusiasms	moaning nematode
button mold	nervous monad
manly nimrod	mistress mine
mean gnome	honorable mention
common denominator	mum nun
main nemesis	numb mummer

5. The words below are not properly matched. Pronounce each word in the left-hand column; then write its number next to its phonetic counterpart.

1. meal	_____ mæstɚ		1. now	_____ nɛvɚ
2. mass	_____ mænlaɪk		2. new	_____ naɪt
3. magnum	_____ mɪd		3. neither	_____ nʌt
4. master	_____ mil		4. nit	_____ naɪs
5. mid	_____ mædɚ		5. nut	_____ naʊ
6. manlike	_____ mɪlkwid		6. nook	_____ niðɚ
7. madder	_____ mæt		7. never	_____ nɪt
8. met	_____ mæs		8. night	_____ nʊk
9. milkweed	_____ mɛt		9. nice	_____ nu
10. mat	_____ mægnəm		10. nip	_____ nɪp

6. Recite as quickly as possible with accuracy:

> If many men knew
> What many men know,

If many men went
Where many men go,
If many men did
What many men do,
The world would be better,
I think so,—don't you?

—MOTHER GOOSE

There was a man in our town,
He couldn't pay his rent;
And so one lonely moonlight night,
To another town he went.

—MOTHER GOOSE

7. Look up the following words in your hardcovered dictionary. Next to each word write its diacritical equivalent and the first definition given. All of these words will be found in the reading below.

	DIACRITICS	DEFINITIONS
Mozart		
Mendelssohn		
Mussorgsky		
Monteverdi		
Menotti		
moribund		
morose		
mussy		
mantle		
melodrama		
mendacious		
Mephistophelean		
mirabile dictu		
mesmerizing		
meter		
mottled		
mousse		
marzipan		
mulligatawny		

moiety   _____   _____
Mohegans   _____   _____
mezzanine   _____   _____
mezzo   _____   _____
metronomes   _____   _____
mocha   _____   _____
Minotaur   _____   _____
medieval   _____   _____

8. Read the following slowly for accuracy. In subsequent readings, try for interpretation and expression.

Mozart, Mendelssohn, Mussorgsky, Monteverdi, and Menotti met in Munich to manufacture a musical masterwork for a modern model of a major metropolis.

"A march!" Mussorgsky muttered into his Munich mug.

"My, my, a march is for moribund, morose morons. I motion that we musicalize a mass!" moaned Mozart from the midst of his mussy, musty mantle.

"Melody, molten melody, is a must! Much melody makes many men merry!" mused Monteverdi.

"My musical mates, music needs melodrama. Music moves men mostly in melodramatic moments, like motion pictures. Musical movies make mesmerizing moments!" marvelled Menotti.

"Meter in music means motion! Meter is momentous! Meter is meaningful! Mustn't mind melodrama; mind meter!" maintained Mendelssohn.

Moustachioed, Mussorgsky mouthed a mountainous, mouldy, mottled mousse, while Mozart mounted a mound of marzipan and marshmallow, mixing on a mortarboard a mess of mushrooms, moose meat balls, moistened with a mulligatawny mush. Nearby, a moiety of Mohegans mixed with a mob of Mohammedans mobilizing in a mass of marigolds and mayonnaise in a murky mezzanine, where a Mexican mezzo mooed to a multitude of metronomes while a mocha-mouthed Minotaur munched milk toast, fed to him by merry mermaids moving to the music of medieval, mcndacious, Mephistophelean monks. Mirabile dictu, this misadventure might move mummies to mambo.

9. Look up the following words in your hardcovered dictionary. Next to each word write its diacritical equivalent and the first definition given.

	DIACRITICS	DEFINITIONS
Nabokov		
nympholeptic		
nymphets		
necromancy		
nolo contendere		
naysaying		
Nietzsche		
neophytes		
nosegays		
non compos mentis		
ninny		
nubile		
novices		
Nostradamus		
noisome		
nincompoop		
Nesselrode		
neutrons		
nectar		
nonce		
nirvana		
nimbus		
neighed		
nonagenarians		
noggins		

10. Read the following slowly for accuracy. In subsequent readings, try for interpretation and expression.

Nabokov, a nimble nightwalker and a natural nympholeptic, nodded his noodle north-northeast, notifying a nest of naked nymphets to navigate for a night of naughty necromancy. Nearby, nolo contendere Ninon neighed, "Nay! Not necessary for nonviolent, naked nymphets to notably display navel and nipple to the nosy neighborhood!"

Naysaying Nietzsche nixed Ninon, "Neophytes need not wear nosegays nor negligees! Nobody, not even a non compos mentis ninny, would nudge naked nymphets into nightshirts! No! Not even Neopolitans, Navahos, or Northumbrians on the nippiest of nights would neglect to notice that nimble footed, nubile novices neglected nighties! Nohow! Noway!"

At high noon a notary public named Nostradamus, a noisome nincompoop, neurotic and nondescript, nose-dived into a nest of Nesselrode, nuts, and nectarines nudging a nearby nuclear bomb into the nymphets' nursery. Nevertheless, the nuclear fusion neglected to negotiate neutrons which were napping and nestling in a nutritious nectar in the nymphets' navels.

In a nonce, no nonsense nannies needled the nymphets into nearby nunneries, nudging Nabokov, Ninon, Nietzsche, and the notary into the nearest nirvana-bound nimbus.

"Nighty-night, night owls!" neighed the nonagerarians.

Then the naughty nannies nipped noggins of nitroglycerin and took needed naps.

EXERCISE 20
[ŋ] *Sounds*

It is important in the pronunciation of this nasal consonant to avoid ending it with a glottal stop, a sound that can best be understood by mispronouncing the words *Long Island* as *Lon Gisland* or *going* as *goin-gah*. The glottal stop occurs when the vocal cords are closed abruptly on the [ŋ]. Do not close the vocal cords; and pronounce the consonant softly as one syllable, not as two.

CHART 6-5. The IPA Consonant Nasal [ŋ].

IPA Symbol	Sample	Type	Tongue	Lips or Mouth	Vocal Cords
ŋ	si*ng*	voiced nasal	tip behind bottom front teeth, back pressed firmly against soft palate, forcing air through nose	slightly open	vibrating

1. Recite each line three times, avoiding a glottal stop and holding the [ŋ] sound for four seconds:

    [ŋ]-ah   [ŋ]-ah   [ŋ]-ah   [ŋ]-ah
    [ŋ]-ah   [ŋ]-ah   [ŋ]-ah   [ŋ]-ah
    [ŋ]-ah   [ŋ]-ah   [ŋ]-ah   [ŋ]-ah
    [ŋ]-ah   [ŋ]-ah   [ŋ]-ah   [ŋ]-ah

2. Pronounce the following words containing [ŋ], holding the [ŋ] for four seconds and avoiding the glottal stop:

Initial	Medial	Final
No words begin with this sound.	springing	ping
	kingdom	gang
	banging	meaning
	singly	laughing
	hanger	squeaking
	belonging	humming

3. Slowly pronounce the following words which contain [ŋ]:

strangling hangman	zinging slingshot
jingling bangle	wangling ranger
longing hunger	singing jingle
jungle living	thronging youngly
ring finger	single sibling
mangling gangrene	sweltering bungalow
staggering wrangler	bungling tangle
narrowing angle	gangling stranger

4. Recite as quickly as possible with accuracy:

Retreating and beating and meeting and sheeting,
Delaying and straying and playing and spraying,
Advancing and prancing and glancing and dancing,
Recoiling, turmoiling and toiling and boiling,
And gleaming and streaming and steaming and beaming,
And rushing and flushing and brushing and gushing,
And flapping and rapping and clapping and slapping,
And curling and whirling and purling and twirling,
And thumping and plumping and bumping and jumping,
And dashing and flashing and splashing and clashing;
And so never ending, but always descending,
Sounds and motions for ever and ever are blending,
All at once and all o'er, with a mighty uproar:
And this way the water comes down at Lodore.

—ROBERT SOUTHEY
The Cataract of Lodore

'Lady Jingly! Lady Jingly!
Sitting where the pumpkins blow,
Will you come and be my wife?'
Said the Yonghy-Bonghy-Bó.
'I am tired of living singly,—
On this coast so wild and shingly,—

I'm a-weary of my life:
If you'll come and be my wife,

Quite serene would be my life!'—
Said the Yonghy-Bonghy-Bó,
Said the Yonghy-Bonghy-Bó.

—EDWARD LEAR

The Courtship of the Yonghy-Bonghy-Bó

5. Match each word below with its correct phonetic counter-part. Sound each pair.

1. shooting _____ lutŋ
2. dumping _____ gɪvŋ
3. shouting _____ sɪŋ
4. loving _____ lʊkŋ
5. looting _____ itŋ
6. giving _____ tʃitŋ
7. seeing _____ dʌmpŋ
8. looking _____ ʃautŋ
9. eating _____ lʌvŋ
10. cheating _____ ʃutŋ

6. This exercise includes no vocabulary drill. Read slowly for accuracy. In subsequent readings, try for interpretation and expression.

Infancy is: breathing, crying, sucking, gurgling, yowling, cooing, burping, digesting, sleeping, growing, seeing, hearing, vomiting, clasping, crawling, biting, smiling, teething, napping, laughing, screaming, demanding, scratching, spilling, ripping, gnawing, finding, stuffing, pointing, toddling, falling, wetting, defecating, bathing.

Childhood is: running, climbing, connecting, talking, discovering, hugging, kissing, teasing, pushing, punching, eating, drinking, hiding, poking, watching, absorbing, retreating, blushing, fearing, attacking, schooling, writing, adding, spelling, daring, testing, praying, cursing, lying, cheating, helping, carrying, hurting, dropping, playing, trusting, coloring, picking, peeling, experiencing, boasting, admiring, adoring, tasting, needing, becoming, growing, changing.

Adolescence is: attracting, grooming, dressing, shampooing, dating, dancing, devising, doing, planning, failing, doubting, dreaming, succeeding, crying, loving, trusting, communicating, desiring, asserting, disobeying, confronting, evaluating, rejecting, joining, touching, hating, risking, swimming, skiing, boating, driving, traveling, searching, meeting, choosing, leaving, going, coming, departing, seeking, finding, questioning.

Middle age is: drudging, repeating, securing, singing, paying, marrying, whispering, creating, painting, sculpting, writing, building, working, sharing, promising, devoting, composing, yelling, divorcing, fattening, criticising, visiting, buying, destroying, healing, praising, overlooking, shooting, voting, bombing, exploiting, preaching, balancing, judging, cooking, selling, seducing, baking, researching, legislating, rubbing, cutting, compromising, accepting, splitting, fishing, partying, dancing, vomiting, over-eating, drinking, telephoning, letter-writing, commanding, teaching, burying, policing, protecting, rapping, competing, depositing, withdrawing, procreating, envying, commending.

Old age is: fulfilling, completing, rounding, arriving, satisfying, enjoying, sharing, advising, self-pitying, self-sacrificing, hardening, softening, applauding, spitting, slowing, stooping, accepting, wrinkling, assisting, caring, worshiping, doddering, mourning, resigning, isolating, recollecting, detaching, dying.

7

IPA Consonants: Fricatives

The IPA consonant fricatives are sounds that are produced by a restricted air flow, resulting in vocal friction. Fricatives include both voiced and voiceless sounds. *Voiced* fricatives include [v], [ð], [z], and [ʒ]. *Voiceless* fricatives include [f], [θ], [s], [ʃ], and [h]. As with plosives, the pairs of sounds in the fricative family have the same lip, mouth, and tongue positions. They differ only in being voiced or voiceless.

CHART 7-1. The IPA Fricatives [v] and [f].

IPA Symbol	Sample	Type	Tongue	Lips or Mouth	Vocal Cords
v	*v*ery	voiced fricative	neutral	upper teeth on lower lip	vibrating
f	*f*ull	unvoiced fricative			non-vibrating

EXERCISE 21
[v] and [f] Sounds
See Chart 7–1

1. During the following, place the hand on the throat to feel
the vocal cords vibrating for [v] and not vibrating for [f].
Recite each horizontal and vertical group three times,
holding the sound marked by parentheses for four seconds:

[v]ah	[v]ah	[v]ah	[v]ah
[f]ah	[f]ah	[f]ah	[f]ah
[v]ah	[v]ah	[v]ah	[v]ah
[f]ah	[f]ah	[f]ah	[f]ah

2. Pronounce the following words containing [v], holding
the [v] for four seconds:

Initial	Medial	Final
very	evict	chive
view	evidence	strive
vireo	eventual	save
vault	livid	leave
victory	review	dove
victim	leaven	groove

3. Pronounce the following words containing [f], holding the
[f] for four seconds:

Initial	Medial	Final
falter	affair	doff
famous	inflame	laugh
famine	confuse	half
future	infer	skiff
fool	reflect	huff
full	rift	quaff

4. To feel the distinction between [v] and [f], read aloud the following pairs of words:

famous wives	stiff victim
faltering dive	fierce raven
strive for	very rough
chive-filled	vast favor
frantic hive	violet fluff
drive fast	favorite vegetable
vivid fancy	variable friend
vicious laugh	votive perfume

5. Match each word below with its correct phonetic counterpart. Sound each pair.

1. fleet _____ fom	1. vote _____ vɪktəri
2. float _____ fɪst	2. very _____ vum
3. fit _____ frʌnt	3. vim _____ væst
4. fill _____ flɪvɚ	4. victim _____ væri
5. from _____ frəm	5. victory _____ vɛri
6. foam _____ fɪt	6. voom _____ vot
7. phone _____ flit	7. void _____ vɪm
8. fist _____ flot	8. vast _____ vɪktɪm
9. front _____ fɪl	9. vary _____ vju
10. flivver _____ fon	10. view _____ void

6. Recite as quickly as possible with accuracy:

> Frivolous Freddy Fish
> Flipped feverishly in his bed,
> For vivid visions of Velma
> Flashed in his fishy head.
>
> Velma, the velvety vamp
> Viscously veered and fled
> From Fred in the fishy damp
> As he flipped on his feverish bed.

7. Look up the following words in your hardcovered dictionary. Next to each word write its diacritical equivalent and the first definition given. All of these words will be found in the reading below.

	DIACRITICS	DEFINITIONS
Florentinians		
Fabians		
forestall		
foreordained		
forebodings		
foreshadowings		
fibrillations		
filigreed		
furbelowed		
farthingales		
fluegelhorns		
florid		
fleur-de-lis		
festooned		
funiculars		
fenestrated		
four-posters		
fratricidal		
Freudians		
flourishing		
floriferous		
frangipani		
fusillade		
forestalled		
fatalistic		
fecund		
fakirs		
flaneurs		
flimflammery		
flying buttress		
fiord		
flotsam		

8. Read the following slowly for accuracy. In subsequent readings, try for interpretation and expression.

Fifty Florentinians, all Fabians, to forestall foreordained forebodings, fierce and foul foreshadowings, which forecast frequent forced feedings and formidable, frantic fibrillations, freed themselves from the flash of freezing fear by forming a free thinkers' federation.

Furnished with filigreed, furbelowed farthingales and frockcoats, plus fluegelhorns, fine-bred phillies, fluorescent fixtures, and fifty-five Frisbees for flinging, they flounced into forty-four florid, fleur-de-lis-festooned funiculars. Each funicular was fenestrated and fitted with four-posters filled with fraternities of fratriciding Freudians, flourishing floriferous frangipani.

Freakishly, a fusillade of flirty, fancy-free, fun-loving, footballers forced themselves, in the fair forenoon, into the forestalled funiculars. Each was fraternally and fetally fixed to a Freudian!

The fatalistic Freudians fled the footballers, fearing fatal fratricidal fatigue as well as frustrating a fecund, fratricidal frolic! Fortunately, flocks of foxy fakirs, all flaneurs, with the finest fingers in all flimflammery, filed into the funicular, fanning the fleeing Freudians and the fainting footballers with flammable flamingo feathers.

The fibrillating Florentinians followed the fleeing Freudians by forming a flying buttress which flung the footballers into a flooding fiord filled with flotsam!

9. Look up the following words or phrases in your hardcovered dictionary. Next to each word write its diacritical equivalent and the first definition given. All of these words will be found in the reading below.

	DIACRITICS	DEFINITIONS
votarized	_____	_____
vigilant	_____	_____

verdant

verified

velocipedes

vivisected

vermillion

venal

valetudinarian

varicose

valorous

antivivisectionist

vitriolic

versifiers

vaunted

vatic

vestal virgins

valedictorians

vituperation

vulgar

vernacular

vamoose

venial

in vino veritas

10. Read the following slowly for accuracy. In subsequent readings, try for interpretation and expression.

Votarized, vigilant vegetarians volunteered to voyage to verdant Venus, where varieties of vineyards were veiled and voided by vapors from vacuous volcanoes. This vintage visit verified for the vigilant vegetarians that very vile, vicious vampires on velvet velocipedes vivisected vermillion vegetables. This venal, vegetal violence was viewed via videovision on Valentine's Day in Venice with a voice-over by a valetudinarian ventriloquist with varicose veins.

The valorous antivivisectionist vegetarians vowed vitriolic vengeance on the vermillion-visaged Venusian vampires. Vehement vegetarian versifiers vaunted volumes of vatic verses as vestal virgins vocalized vespers with vain-glorious valedictorians in vigil-lighted vestibules.

The villainous vampires vented vigorous vituperation in a vulgar vernacular. "Vamoose, vigorless and venial vege-tarians. Verily, not only do Venusian vampires vivisect vegetables, but we violate varieties of vines in our vast vats under vicious vices. Vulgar vines are vanished to vinegar vats! The best vines become vino! Et in vino veritas! Vamoose!"

CHART 7-2. The IPA Consonant Fricatives [ð] and [θ].

IPA Symbol	Sample	Type	Tongue	Lips or Mouth	Vocal Cords
ð	*th*at	voiced fricative	tip between teeth or behind upper front teeth	neutral	vibrating
θ	*th*ink	unvoiced fricative			non-vibrating

Some persons confuse [t] and [d] sounds with [ð] and [θ]: for example, *dis* for *this*, *dat* for *that*, *tink* for *think*. If you have this problem, make sure in pronouncing [ð] and [θ] that your tongue tip is placed between the teeth. Do not protrude tongue.

EXERCISE 22
[ð] *and* [θ] *Sounds*

1. Making sure that your tongue tip is between your teeth, recite each horizontal and vertical group three times, hold-ing the bracketed sound for four seconds:

[ð]a   [d]a   [ð]a   [t]a

[θ]a   [d]a   [θ]a   [t]a

[ð]a [d]a [ð]a [t]a
[θ]a [d]a [θ]a [t]a

2. Pronounce the following words containing [ð], holding the [ð] for four seconds:

Initial	Medial	Final
this	without	bathe
then	rather	writhe
those	mother	breathe
there	other	smooth
that	another	soothe
the	smoother	teethe

3. Pronounce the following words containing [θ], holding the [θ] for four seconds:

Initial	Medial	Final
thought	birthday	growth
thank	anything	girth
thick	something	fifth
through	deathless	faith
thigh	mirthless	math
thumb	toothless	moth

4. To feel the distinction between [ð], [θ], [d], and [t], read aloud the following pairs of words:

opinionated theme	blighted thistles
dimpled thighs	seething throng
doubted myth	worthy thane
writhing demon	thin batter
tidy father	offered thanks
fitted thimble	tired mother
volatile thoughts	bold Theodore
bloated thumb	mild Thaddeus

5. Match each word below with its correct phonetic counterpart. Sound each pair.

1. thee _____ əðɚ
2. hither _____ brʌðɚ
3. rather _____ 'gæðɚ
4. breathes _____ 'læðz
5. thou _____ 'zɪðɚ
6. other _____ ræðɚ
7. brother _____ ði
8. gather _____ 'hɪðɚ
9. lather _____ briðz
10. zither _____ ðaʊ

1. thigh _____ θɔt
2. think _____ bæθ
3. wrath _____ mɪθ
4. path _____ wɪdθ
5. thought _____ θɪnk
6. bath _____ læθ
7. myth _____ θaɪ
8. width _____ mæθ
9. lath _____ pæθ
10. math _____ ræθ

6. Recite as quickly as possible with accuracy:

> Theophilus Thistle, the successful thistle sifter, in sifting a sieveful of unsifted thistles, thrust three thousand thistles through the thick of his thumb. Now if Theophilus Thistle, the successful thistle sifter, in sifting a sieveful of unsifted thistles, thrust three thousand thistles through the thick of his thumb, see that thou, in sifting a sieveful of unsifted thistles, thrust not three thousand thistles through the thick of thy thumb. Success to the successful thistle sifter!

—ANON

7. Look up the following words in your hardcovered dictionary. Next to each word write its diacritical equivalent and the first definition given. All of these words will be found in the reading below.

	DIACRITICS	DEFINITIONS
Thais	_____	_____
Thaumaturgic	_____	_____
Thalia	_____	_____

Thor	_____	_____
theocratic	_____	_____
Theocritus	_____	_____
thespian	_____	_____
Thespis	_____	_____
thermal	_____	_____
think-tank	_____	_____
thin-skinnedness	_____	_____
thaumatologically	_____	_____
third world	_____	_____
third parties	_____	_____
third-dimensional	_____	_____
thesaurus	_____	_____
thanes	_____	_____
theomorphic	_____	_____
thermonuclear	_____	_____

8. Read the following slowly for accuracy. In subsequent readings, try for interpretation and expression.

Thick-skinned Thais, thaumaturgic Thalia, thumping Thor, theocratic Theocritus, and theatre's thoroughbred thespian, Thespis, thronged on Thursdays, or thereabouts, while threadbare, thrush-throated theologians thanked their theoretical theologies for not being thankless third-raters!

Therefore, thereby, therewith, and thereupon they threw themselves into a thick, thermal, thriving think-tank, thinking that thin-skinnedness is thaumatologically and theoretically thought to be thrivingly better for third world, third persons, third parties, or thought-thirsty, thorough-going, third dimensional, thrifty, throbbing, throttle-throwing, thugs like themselves!

Thespis threw thimbles, thingamajigs, and thingama-bobs as well as this thought to the thesaurus-thrashing throng of over thirteen thinkers: "Fellow thugs, think! Oh, thanes of thrills and thievery, would not a thousand theomorphic thermonuclear thunderclaps be a thoroughly theatrical thriller!"

CHART 7-3. The IPA Fricatives [z] and [s].

IPA Symbol	Sample	Type	Tongue	Lips or Mouth	Vocal Cords
z	zoom	voiced fricative	tongue grooved with sides touching upper teeth and gums, tongue tip slightly re-moved from upper gum ridge or from behind lower teeth to allow a fine stream of air to flow	neutral	vibrating
s	sea	unvoiced fricative			non-vibrating

EXERCISE 23

[Z] and [S] Sounds

1. Opening mouth wide on each sound, repeat each horizontal and vertical group three times, always holding the bracketed sound for four seconds:

[z]ah	[z]ah	[z]ah	[z]ah
[s]ah	[s]ah	[s]ah	[s]ah
[z]ah	[z]ah	[z]ah	[z]ah
[s]ah	[s]ah	[s]ah	[s]ah

2. Pronounce the following words containing [z], holding the [z] for four seconds:

Initial	Medial	Final
zip	hazy	quiz
zest	measles	prize

zeal	marzipan	buzz
zoo	breezy	was
zone	ozone	as
zag	fuzzy	cause

3. Pronounce the following words containing [s], holding the [s] for four seconds:

Initial	Medial	Final
stroke	misspell	race
strict	massive	mass
sing	pastime	this
smog	lesser	recess
strum	rustic	boss
sting	tussle	six

4. To feel the distinction between [z] and [s], read aloud the following pairs of words:

lacy daisy	does once
diced raisins	Swiss cheese
nice nose	summer breeze
teased tresses	easy aces
pleasing place	hazy skies
busy bus	raspberry ice
graceful fleas	mystic Aztec
lazy lassie	minstrel music

5. Match each word below with its correct phonetic counterpart. Sound each pair.

1. sum _____ ston	1. zoo _____ zulu
2. saw _____ sten	2. zipper _____ zibrə
3. swim _____ staʊt	3. zeal _____ zɛfɚ
4. street _____ 'strænɡɚ	4. Zulu _____ zæni
5. stout _____ sɔ	5. zigzag _____ zo
6. stranger _____ sʌm	6. zebra _____ zɪro
7. stain _____ swɪm	7. zephyr _____ zɪnk
8. stone _____ strit	8. zany _____ zigzæg

9. sister _____ stupɪd
10. stupid _____ 'sɪstɚ

9. zero _____ zɪpɚ
10. zinc _____ zil

6. Recite as quickly as possible with accuracy:

> Swan swam over the sea—
> Swim, swan, swim;
> Swan swam back again,
> Well swum, swan.

> If you sneeze on Monday, you sneeze for danger;
> Sneeze on a Tuesday, kiss a stranger;
> Sneeze on a Wednesday, sneeze for a letter;
> Sneeze on a Thursday, something better;
> Sneeze on a Friday, sneeze for sorrow;
> Sneeze on a Saturday, see your sweetheart tomorrow.

> —MOTHER GOOSE

7. Look up the following words in your hardcovered diction-
    ary. Next to each word write its diacritical equivalent and
    the first definition given. All of these words will be found
    in the reading below.

	DIACRITICS	DEFINITIONS
solstice		
sidereal		
syncopation		
sextillion		
sexagenarian		
septuagenarian		
suffragettes		
sojourned		
supernumeraries		
stentorian		
serendipity		
stagnant		

stygian

seraglio

stalactites

stalagmites

stratified

soporific

somnolent

sotto voce

Spartan

sedate

separatist

scherzo

Scriabin

supine

Segovia

scrumptious

smorgasbord

salvers

George Sand

Sabine

Sappho

senile

samurai

Sophocles

Solomon

Socrates

sapient

sine qua non

symposium

semantics

sybaritic

sanguinary

sylvan

Stone of Scone

serape

Sephardic

sacerdotal

satyrs

sachets

8. Read the following slowly for accuracy. In subsequent readings, try for interpretation and expression.

As the summer solstice swished in sidereal syncopation, a sextillion sexagenarian and septuagenarian suffragettes sojourned simultaneously, like supernumeraries in a stentorian, singsong, swarm scene, with splendid serendipity, into a stagnant, stultifying, stygian seraglio, spoked with stalactites and stalagmites!!

There steeped in stratified, soporific, and somnolent sensuality, skeletonized sisters slaved in squalor! Singing sotto voce, the Spartan suffragettes sped their sisters of the seraglio into the sunshine of a sedate salon, not a stuffy separatist saloon, where a symphonic scherzo of Scriabin was being played by a supine Segovia through a sterling stethoscope. A scrumptious smorgasbord on silver salvers was served by George Sand and the Sabine sisterhood while Sappho satirized senile samurai. Sophocles, Solomon, and Socrates later led a sapient, sine qua non symposium on the semantics of sybaritic statesmen, sanguinary Santas, and the seduction and servitude of sensitized saints.

Later in a sylvan setting, surrounding the Stone of Scone, sassafras tea and sarsaparilla were spooned out by ex-swinging, serapied scoundrels of the Spanish Sephardic school of separatism assisted by several sacerdotal separatist specialists from the Sacred City. Several satyrs, in sackcloth, strewed sachets to the satisfied sisters.

9. Look up the following words in your hardcovered dictionary. Next to each word write its diacritical equivalent and the first definition given. All of these words will be found in the reading for this exercise.

	DIACRITICS	DEFINITIONS
zonked		
Zarathustra		
zoophilic		
von Zeppelin		

zigzagged	_____	_____
zeniths	_____	_____
Efrem Zimbalist	_____	_____
Zeno	_____	_____
zirconned	_____	_____
zither	_____	_____
Florenz Ziegfeld	_____	_____
zodiac	_____	_____
zoot suited	_____	_____
zeitgeist	_____	_____
Zen	_____	_____
zealots	_____	_____
zany	_____	_____
zombies	_____	_____
Zechariah	_____	_____
Zoroaster	_____	_____
zoanthropic	_____	_____
Zeus	_____	_____
Zionistic	_____	_____
zwieback	_____	_____
zabaglione	_____	_____
zucchini	_____	_____
woozy	_____	_____
zephyr	_____	_____
zero gravity	_____	_____

10. Read the following slowly for accuracy. In subsequent readings, try for interpretation and expression.

Thus spoke a zonked Zarathustra, as he zippered up and a zebra striped zeppelin, commandeered by the zoophilic von Zeppelin, zigzagged above the zeniths of Zanzibar, Zambia, and the Zuider Zee! "Let Efrem Zimbalist zap away on a zinc fiddle, while Zeno zings on a zirconned zither, and Florenz Ziegfeld directs the zodiac zoo in a zowie zoot-suited chorus line. The zeitgeist has zeroed on Zen! Zen with zest! Zen with zing! Zounds! What this zone known as earth needs are millions of zapping Zen zealots!" Just then zany zombies led by Zechariah, Zoroaster, and a zoanthropic Zeus, served Zionistic zwieback soaked with zabaglione on zucchini, as von Zeppelin's zeppelin lazily rose in a woozy zephyr, and Zarathustra zoomed off with Zeno before zero gravity zapped them up. Zilch!

CHART 7-4. The IPA Consonant Fricatives [ʒ] and [ʃ].

IPA Symbol	Sample	Type	Tongue	Lips or Mouth	Vocal Cords
ʒ	measure	voiced fricative	tip to upper gum ridge or behind lower front teeth, tongue flatter and lower than for [s] or [z], sides of tongue pressed against upper side teeth	neutral	vibrating
ʃ	shell	unvoiced fricative			non vibrating

EXERCISE 24
[ʒ] and [ʃ] Sounds

1. Comparing tongue position with that for [z] and [s], and noting the slight differences, repeat each horizontal and vertical group three times, always holding the bracketed sound for four seconds:

[ʒ]ah	[ʒ]ah	[ʒ]ah	[ʒ]ah
[ʃ]ah	[ʃ]ah	[ʃ]ah	[ʃ]ah
[ʒ]ah	[ʒ]ah	[ʒ]ah	[ʒ]ah
[ʃ]ah	[ʃ]ah	[ʃ]ah	[ʃ]ah

2. Pronounce the following words containing [ʒ], holding the [ʒ] for four seconds:

Initial	Medial	Final
No words	illusion	rouge
begin with	elysian	massage
this sound.	conversion	mirage
	azure	garage
	negligee	prestige
	decision	corsage

3. Pronounce the following words containing [ʃ], holding the [ʃ] for four seconds:

Initial	Medial	Final
shell	motion	plush
shall	national	wish
should	fished	hashish
shop	meshed	rash
sheep	machine	flesh
shape	ocean	squash

4. To feel the distinction between [ʒ] and [ʃ], read aloud the following pairs of words:

Confucian confusion	rash euthanasia
ashen Asian	plushy pleasure
unleashed leisure	fish measure
garage machine	treasured wish
azure threshold	shah's taj
fresh version	lush fusion
lush mirage	bishop's largesse
blush rouge	massaged flesh

5. Match each word below with its correct phonetic counterpart. Sound each pair.

1. dish _____ pærɪʃ
2. nourish _____ hæʃ
3. dash _____ flæʃ
4. wish _____ pæʃən
5. parish _____ waʃ
6. hash _____ ʌpʃɑt
7. flash _____ wɪʃ
8. passion _____ dæʃ
9. wash _____ dɪʃ
10. upshot _____ 'nɚɪʃ

1. division _____ beʒ
2. derision _____ 'plɛʒɚ
3. television _____ 'æʒɚ
4. beige _____ də'vɪʒən
5. pleasure _____ ə'vɚʒən
6. azure _____ dɪrɪʒən
7. leisure _____ supɚ'vɪʒən
8. aversion _____ 'tɛləvɪʒən
9. supervision _____ 'profjuʒən
10. profusion _____ 'liʒɚ

6. Recite as quickly as possible with accuracy:

> Missy Mashy loved her pleasure;
> Missy Mashy loved her leisure;
> Missy Mashy had no illusion;
> Missy Mashy was no Confucian.

7. The sound [ʒ] is not found in the initial position. Pronounce the following words in which it is contained.

casually	bludgeon	confusion
seizure	mirage	delusion
beige	sabotage	lesion
measure	intrusion	malnutrition
television	rouge	collision
derision	infusion	bijoux
leisure	vision	explosion
treasure	fusion	erosion
contusion	convulsion	enclosure
ambrosia	division	Polynesian

8. Look up the following words in your hardcovered dictionary. Next to each word write its diacritical equivalent and the first definition given. All of these words will be found in the reading for this exercise.

	DIACRITICS	DEFINITIONS
shofar	_____	_____
shysters	_____	_____
shorn	_____	_____
shillelaghs	_____	_____
Shaw	_____	_____
Shelley	_____	_____
Sheridan	_____	_____
Shostakovich	_____	_____
shish kebob	_____	_____
Ted Shawn	_____	_____
Shinto	_____	_____
shamans	_____	_____
shrike	_____	_____
shingle	_____	_____
shallots	_____	_____
shoo-in	_____	_____
shellacking	_____	_____
shrove	_____	_____
shimmied	_____	_____
sashayed	_____	_____
Shangri-la	_____	_____
shibboleths	_____	_____

9. Read the following slowly for accuracy. In subsequent reading, try for interpretation and expression.

The shofar sent shuddering shivers through the shanties of Sheboygan and Shaker Heights. Shameless shopkeepers shuttered their shops as the shofar once more sent its shock waves shushing all shop talk! Shazam! The showdown shut down the shysters' showcases. Even show business sharks showing "Sharks" sheepishly shut down their shipshape "Shark" shows.

Shorn, shirtwaisted, shaggy, sharp-nosed, short-tempered, sporting shillelaghs and shiners, came Shakespeare, Shaw, Shelley and Sheridan. Shostakovich conducted with a shish kebob for a baton while Ted Shawn and some Shinto shamans shouldered the show's shimmering shindig showpiece.

Onto the stage, a shrike-strewn shingle, came Shakespeare. "Shaw, you Shavian shrimp, strike!"

Vegetarian Shaw, shamed and shackled by a shopping bag full of shallots, shouted to Shelley and Sheridan, "Shape up, you shammers!"

"Shalom, shalom," they shyly, shamefacedly stammered when sly Shelley shouldered a shortcake straight at Shakespeare's shaven skull. The shortcake seemed a shoo-in, but streaked like a shooting star into Shakespeare's shoeshine! Suddenly a shower of shamrocks and shallots shimmered all over the shingle.

A shorn shaveling named Shirley Temple showed Shakespeare, Shaw, Shelley, and Sheridan into the shelter of the Sheraton Sheffield, after the shellacking, for sherbets. All shrove and for penance shampooed Shetland sheep dogs till they shone.

All shimmied as they sashayed to Shangri-la, shouting shocking shibboleths!

CHART 7-5. The IPA Consonant Fricative [h].

IPA Symbol	Sample	Type	Tongue	Lips or Mouth	Vocal Cords
h	how	unvoiced fricative	poised to move into position for next sound	poised to go into position for next sound	partly open to permit passage of air as in whispering and non-vibrating

EXERCISE 25

[h] Sound

The [h] sound is almost not a separate sound. The articulators are set to make the next sound, but breath is blown through the vocal cords before the next sound begins. Many Americans do not sound the [h] in words like *humor*, *humble*, *humid*, *humility*, *human*, *humanity*. However, the [h] sound should be made before these words. There are exceptions. *Heir*, for instance—derived from French, which has no sounded [h]— is pronounced *air*. *Homage*, also from the French, can be pronounced with or without the [h], although first preference goes to a pronunciation without it. *Forehead* can also be pronounced either way, and again first preference goes to a pronunciation without the [h]. If you are in any doubt whether to sound the [h] in a word, consult a dictionary.

1. For practice, exaggerate each position of the articulators and each sound and do not try to hold the [h] for four seconds, as you recite each horizontal and vertical group three times:

      [h]ah   [h]ay   [h]ee   [h]oo
      [h]oo   [h]ee   [h]ay   [h]ah
      [h]ee   [h]oo   [h]ah   [h]ay
      [h]ay   [h]ah   [h]oo   [h]ee

2. Pronounce the following words containing the sound [h]:

Initial	Medial	Final
heat	nihilist	no words
hill	neighborhood	end with
how	priesthood	this sound.
help	unhinge	
hip	superhuman	
hope	inhabit	

3. Pronounce the following words containing [h]:

howling hurricane	Hounslow Heath
handsome hound	helping hand
hallowed hollow	hard hoof
hungry hawk	harbor haven
humid heat	heavenly harp
huge hippo	hearty hamper
hairy head	heedless hurry
hot haste	hundred herrings

4. Match each word below with its correct phonetic counterpart. Sound each pair.

1. health _____ hɪd
2. hello _____ hæŋ
3. hilly _____ hibru
4. howl _____ hɛlkæt
5. hull _____ hʊre
6. hooray _____ hɛlθ
7. hid _____ hɛlo
8. hang _____ hɪli
9. Hebrew _____ haʊl
10. hellcat _____ hʌl

5. Recite as quickly as possible with accuracy:

It's not the heavy hauling that hurts the horses' hooves;
It's the hammer, hammer, hammer on the hard highway.

Had a rhino hair on his horn,
He'd hardly behave so horrid;
He'd be happy to have been born
With mohair on his forehead.

6. Look up the following words in your hardcovered dictionary. Next to each word write its diacritical equivalent and the first definition given. The reading in this exercise contains all the words.

	Diacritics	Definitions
Hadrian's Wall		
Hecuba		
heliotrope		
hollandaised		
haggis		
hurly-burly		
hoary		
heath		
hodgepodge		
hobbits		
homogeny		
hydronaut		
habanera		
Handel		
Hindemith		
Heifetz		
hookah		
V. Horowitz		
Anne Hathaway		
Hermann Hesse		
Gerard Manley Hopkins		
haikus		
Lafcadio Hearn		
harried		
Hammurabi		
Herod		
hara-kiri		
hygienic		
hostelry		
historiographers		
Halley's comet		
hominoid		
heinous		
holocausts		

7. Read the following slowly for accuracy. In subsequent readings, try for interpretation and expression.

As a half-moon hovered haltingly over Hadrian's Wall, Hecuba, hiccupping, was helped by a half-witted Humpty Dumpty to heave heliotrope, hollandaised haddocks, hamburgers, haggis and hot dogs into a hurly-burly, hell broth. Huddled beneath them, on the humid, hoary heath, a hodgepodge of humanity, hosts of Hopis, Hasidic Hebrews, Hellenists, hobbits, Hindus, and hobgoblins hallelujahed in a heavenly homogeny.

Hero, the heavy-hearted hanger-on of hydronaut horror, hurled herself into a hokey, hopping-hot habanera. Handel handled the harpsichord, Hindemith howled, and Heifetz inhaled on a hookah. Vladimir Horowitz hummed holy hymns, while Anne Hathaway, Hermann Hesse, and Gerard Manley Hopkins hacked out hare-brained haikus. Lafcadio Hearn helped and harried.

Hammurabi, Herod, and Hamlet hollered histrionically for next at hara-kiri. Hygienic Thomas Hardy hurried about half-cocked, helter-skelter, hush-hushing a hostelry of hellcat hooligans, who had horrible halitosis.

This historiographer's holiday halted when hoards of helicopters hoisted this honorable herd of humanity to hitchhike a heavenly ride on Halley's comet.

Hangdog Hitler, a hominoid of heinous holocausts, was left behind with a harpoon of heavy hydrogen in his horrible heart!

8

IPA Consonants: Semivowels, Glides, Combinations

SEMIVOWELS

IPA *semivowels* are consonant sounds that are less restricted than the fricatives. There are two *voiced* semivowels [l] and [r]. There are no voiceless semivowels.

CHART 8-1. The IPA Consonant Semivowel: [l] Sound

IPA Symbol	Sample	Type	Tongue	Lips or Mouth	Vocal Cords
l	love	voiced semivowel	tip of tongue to upper gum ridge, sides lowered to avoid trapping air	neutral	vibrating

EXERCISE 26
[*l*] Sound

It is important in pronouncing a good [l] to keep the tongue working and in the front of the mouth, rather than farther back. Experiment by producing an [l] with the tongue held alternately to the upper gum ridge and to the center of the hard palate. A good [l] can be produced only in the front of the mouth.

1. Recite each horizontal and vertical group three times, holding the bracketed sound for four seconds:

[l]ah	[l]ay	[l]ee	[l]oo
[l]ay	[l]ee	[l]oo	[l]ah
[l]ee	[l]oo	[l]ah	[l]ay
[l]oo	[l]ah	[l]ay	[l]ee

2. Slowly pronounce the following words containing [l], holding the [l] for four seconds:

Initial	Medial	Final
limpid	hallow	lentil
luxuriate	balloon	knoll
lily	collect	jowl
legibility	plant	veal
lapidary	willow	soul
lever	salt	real

3. To feel the distinction between [l] and [r], read aloud the following pairs of words:

luscious rubies	loathed leper
flute reed	nether longitude
ludicrous rogue	lither lily
rhyming lullaby	lover's letter
truly rural	regal eagle

row lustily   realistic plethora
lovers' leap   frail Thalia
withered willow   flailed lather

4. Match each word below with its correct phonetic counterpart. Sound each pair.

1. null _____ ʃɛl
2. bleed _____ lʌvɪŋli
3. only _____ əlon
4. lost _____ riəlɪ
5. really _____ lɔst

6. long _____ laɪbrɛri
7. lovingly _____ nʌl
8. shell _____ blid
9. alone _____ onli
10. library _____ lɔŋ

5. Recite as quickly as possible with accuracy:

Lettuce! O Lettuce!
Let us, O let us,
O Lettuce leaves,
O let us leave this tree and eat
Lettuce, O let us, Lettuce leaves!

—EDWARD LEAR
*The Story of the Four Little Children
Who Went Round the World*

6. Look up the following words in your hardcovered dictionary. Next to each word write its diacritical equivalent and the first definition given. All of these words are in the reading.

	DIACRITICS	DEFINITIONS
leitmotif		
Lohengrin		
latitudinarian		
libations		
Liebfraumilch		
labyrinthine		
lotus-eaters		

lexicographical   _____   _____
lepidopterists   _____   _____
lapidarians   _____   _____
lithographs   _____   _____
loggerheaded   _____   _____
lauded   _____   _____
Leaning Tower of Pisa   _____   _____
lignified   _____   _____
lobes   _____   _____
lobotomized   _____   _____
lollygagging   _____   _____
lordlings   _____   _____
lip-synced   _____   _____
longitudinally   _____   _____
leprechauns   _____   _____
lubricious   _____   _____
luminescent   _____   _____
lacerated   _____   _____
lorgnette   _____   _____
latitudinally   _____   _____
leviathan   _____   _____
lethargic   _____   _____
legation   _____   _____
Lottes   _____   _____
Lehmann   _____   _____
Lenya   _____   _____
lachrymose   _____   _____
lentissimo   _____   _____

7. Read the following slowly for accuracy. In subsequent readings, try for interpretation and expression.

"Look, lads and lassies, what a lovely, lopsided landscape!" laughed the loggerheaded lumberjack as he lauded the lean and Leaning Tower of Pisa. His lignified lobes were lately lobotomized. Lollygagging lordlings from Londonderry, Luchow, Lualaba, Los Alamos, and Louisville ludicrously lip-synced the looney lumberjack.

Lo! Longitudinally located on all levels of the leaning

Leaner, loads of lollipop-licking leprechauns lowered lengths of lubricious, luminescent, lacerated ladders of licorice to the lorgnette-leering lordlings. At lecterns located latitudinally on the leaning licorice leviathan, loud-mouthed lecturers lavished loads of lyrics on the lethargic, loopy legation.

From the Leaning Tower's loftiest level Lottes Lehmann and Lenya lullabied the locality with a lachrymose, lentissimo leitmotif from Lohengrin. Latitudinarian luminaries ladled libations of Liebfraumilch laced with lashing lobsters. In a labyrinthine lounge legions of lotus-eaters leafed through lexicographical leaflets. Nearby, lepidopterists and lapidarians, in ligament-loosening lotus positions, lunched on Limburger and limes, while the Lowells, Longfellow, Lorca, Lope de Vega, and the Lake lyricists looked at lent lithographs from the Louvre.

CHART 8-2. The IPA Consonant Semivowel [r].

IPA Symbol	Sample	Type	Tongue	Lips or Mouth	Vocal Cords
r	rub	voiced semivowel	tip of tongue flattened and pointed upward, center arched, sides of tongue touching upper rear teeth	mouth slightly open, lips drawn slightly back	vibrating

EXERCISE 27
[r] Sound

It must be remembered, as with [l], that the tongue has to do the work in the production of the [r] sound. If a lazy tongue is compensated for by the lips, the familiar substitution of [w] for [r] results. Be sure to make your tongue active in the production of both [l] and [r].

This voiced semivowel can cause trouble because it is omitted in some dialects (as in New York City, eastern New England, and parts of the south) and added intrusively in others (New York City, eastern New England). Once you have learned a speech pattern in childhood, you can correct it only with difficulty and hard work.

A common example of the dropped [r] is when the word *for* is incorrectly pronounced *fuh*. In the same way, *her* becomes *huh*. You have probably heard the illustration of Boston dialect for *Park the car in Harvard Yard: Pahk the cah in Hahvahd yahd.*

The intrusive [r] turns up in words like *law (lore)*, *idea (idear)*, *vanilla (vaniller)*. President John Kennedy called attention to this regionalism during the 1961 Cuban missile crisis by his repeated references to *Cuber*.

1. Recite each horizontal and vertical group three times, holding the [r] for four seconds:

[r]ah	[r]ay	[r]ee	[r]oo
[r]ay	[r]ee	[r]oo	[r]ah
[r]ee	[r]oo	[r]ah	[r]ay
[r]oo	[r]ah	[r]ay	[r]ee

2. Slowly pronounce the following words containing [r], holding the [r] for four seconds:

Initial	Medial	Final
rod	rural	huckster
recur	saturate	pioneer
rotund	stratosphere	barber
rumble	lingering	fissure
ruth	horrible	ever
racer	farrow	mar

3. To feel the distinction between [r], [l], and [w], read aloud the following pairs of words:

yellow creamer   wire lyre
rubber pillow   war lore
raucous walk   wool frill
rear window   real weal
royal trowel   raw law
woozy Rosy   low row
large roll   frayed lei
truly rural   waylaid prey

4. Match each word below with its correct phonetic counterpart. Sound each pair.

1. wrote _____ rat   6. raw _____ ruɪn
2. riot _____ rɔ   7. rude _____ res
3. rice _____ rud   8. ruin _____ raɪs
4. race _____ rʌt   9. rut _____ rot
5. rot _____ rɛdbɝd   10. redbird _____ raɪət

5. Recite as quickly as possible with accuracy:

Around the rough and rugged rock the ragged rascal ran.

> Ruby, the riotous witch,
> Was perfectly willing to wed
> A beatnik rebellious and rich
> If broom-borne he'd ride on his head.

6. Look up the following words in your hardcovered dictionary. Next to each word write its diacritical equivalent and the first definition given. These words will also be found in the reading.

	DIACRITICS	DEFINITIONS
revisionist	_____	_____
regenerative	_____	_____
repertory theatre	_____	_____
retrogression	_____	_____
renaissance	_____	_____
rabid	_____	_____

reprimanding   _____   _____
Rumpelstiltskin   _____   _____
rigamarole
repartee
redoubtable
recalcitrant
recidivists
redundant
reverberatory
rhapsodic
renege
rapprochement
redolent
replenished
Romulus and Remus
ruttish
Henri Rousseau
Jacques Rousseau
retainer
Rubaiyat
Rorschach
repugn
ravel
raga
Ryder
Renoir
Rembrandt

7. Read the following slowly for accuracy. In subsequent readings, try for interpretation and expression.

Rumpelstiltskin, a revisionist, radical, regenerative, repertory theatre rabble-rouser, recently revamped and regrouped his rotten repertoire in order to rejuvenate his recent theatrical retrogression. "A repertory renaissance is required to rescue, reinspire, rehabilitate, and replenish this ruinous recession," resounded the rabid, reprimanding Rumpelstiltskin in a recent radio rigamarole repartee.

Redoubtable revolutionaries, all recalcitrant recidivists, responded to this redundant, reverberatory, rhapsodic renunciation ready to rehearse, rehash, renege and restructure the rabid Rumpelstiltskin's rapprochement.

Redolent and responsive, the replenished Rumpelstiltskin in a resounding recitation ran down the repertory's roll call.

"Romulus and Remus!"

"Right!," responded the ravenous, ruttish Romans.

"Rousseau, Henri, and Jacques."

"RIGHT!" they replied.

"Rasputin!"

"Ready, I retail reincarnations and resurrections for a respectable retainer!"

"Rubaiyat!" Rumpelstiltskin recited.

"Retard, retard!" roared the repertory rapscallions, "Rorschach, Rorschach!"

"Rabelais!" retaliated Rumpelstiltskin.

"Rubbish," Rabelais rasped, in repulsion, ready to repugn.

Ravel revamped a raga into a repetitive rackety rhythm as Ryder, Renoir, and Rembrandt repainted recycled remnants from a rancid restaurant.

THE GLIDES

The IPA consonant glides are sounds produced with the articulators in motion. There are both *voiced* and *voiceless* guides. *Voiced* glides include the sounds [w] and [j], whereas the single *voiceless* glide is the [ʍ] sound.

EXERCISE 28
[w] and [ʍ] Sounds

The [ʍ] sound, or *"wh"* (or *"hw,"* as some phoneticians express it), is gradually becoming less current in this country, but it is a nuance still to be recommended to the precise speaker. Many persons would describe Moby Dick as a *wite wale*, but a pronunciation of the [ʍ] sound, made as if you were softly blowing out a candle, is preferable. Pronouncing it in this way will also ensure that it is voiceless, as it should be. If you have difficulty with the sound it may also help if you conceive of it, as some phoneticians do, as a *"hw"* sound, with the [h] sounded first and the [w] second.

CHART 8-3. The IPA Consonant Glides [w] and [ʍ].

IPA Symbol	Sample	Type	Tongue	Lips or Mouth	Vocal Cords
w	*wi*ll	voiced glide	tip behind lower front teeth, back raised toward hard palate, tongue prepared to glide into next sound	rounded in whistling position, then gliding into position for next sound	vibrating
ʍ	*wh*ere	unvoiced glide			non-vibrating

1. Recite each horizontal and vertical group three times, holding the bracketed sound for four seconds:

    [w]ah [w]ah [w]ah [w]ah
    [ʍ]ah [ʍ]ah [ʍ]ah [ʍ]ah

    [w]ah [w]ah [w]ah [w]ah
    [ʍ]ah [ʍ]ah [ʍ]ah [ʍ]ah

2. Slowly pronounce the following words containing [w]:

Initial	*Medial*	*Final*
*w*eep	*w*igwam	No words end with this sound. In
*w*orry	*w*illowy	spite of the presence in English of
*w*ill	*wh*irl*w*ind	words like *willow* and *follow*, the

*wi*tty	*whi*ppoorwill	final consonant *w* is not pro-
*wo*e	re*war*d	nounced, and the word ends for
*wo*o	for*war*d	practical purposes with a vowel

sound. Similarly the ending of the word *cow* is actually the diphthong [aʊ].

3. Slowly pronounce the following words containing [ʍ]:

Initial	*Medial*	*Final*
*wha*ler	mean*whi*le	No words end
*whe*at	bob*whi*te	with this
*whi*p	any*whe*re	sound.
*whe*n	some*wha*t	
*wha*ck	bull*whi*p	
*whe*el	a*whi*le	

4. To feel the distinction between [w] and [ʍ], read aloud the following pairs of words:

whispered reward	white wine
why wield	wailing whippoorwill
wet whale	willing whippet
weep awhile	what wattage
which way	whining walrus
western wheat	witty whelks
wet whetstone	weeping wheezes
woman's whim	whig's wig

5. Match each word below with its correct phonetic counter-part. Sound each pair.

1. wives _____ watʃ	1. whelp _____ ʍupi
2. wishbone _____ waɪf	2. when _____ ʍiz
3. winch _____ wæʃtaʊt	3. whip _____ ʍaɪtfɪʃ
4. wigwag _____ wɔtɚ	4. whether _____ ʍɚl
5. woe _____ wɪdo	5. which _____ ʍɛlp
6. widow _____ wo	6. whisper _____ ʍɛn
7. water _____ wigwæg	7. whoopee _____ ʍɪp

8. washed-out _____ wintʃ
9. wife _____ waɪvz
10. watch _____ wɪʃbon

8. wheeze _____ ʌɛðɚ
9. whitefish _____ ʌɪtʃ
10. whirl _____ ʌɪspɚ

6. Recite as quickly as possible with accuracy:

> Willie, a wheezing, white whale,
> Wed Wilma, a quail that was frail;
> But his wife went awash with a squish and a squash
> When the tail of the whale flailed the quail.

7. Look up the following words in your hardcovered dictionary. Next to each word write its diacritical equivalent and the first definition given. All of these words will be found in the reading for this exercise.

	DIACRITICS	DEFINITIONS
wastrels		
wisenheimers		
wraiths		
whited sepulchers		
will-o'-the-wisps		
whimsical		
womanizers		
wahines		
warped		
wizened		
willy-nilly		
Walden Pond		
warrants		
white dwarf		
warheads		

8. Read the following slowly for accuracy. In subsequent readings, try for interpretation and expression.

A word to the wise!
    A warning to wheedling wastrels, wisenheimers, whoremasters, and warmongers! We the woebegone of a

wobbly, war-torn world are wise to you. We wish to warn you wolves of wicked weaponry that we war wraiths, we women suffragettes, we wasted workers, we the weakened, the weary, the warped of the world, are waking up to your wanton, wacky, whoop-de-doo, wasteful ways.

What, are you wonderstruck that we have withdrawn ourselves from your war and whiskey whirlpool? Woe to you whited sepulchers, we are wise to your whitewashing ways. The whipping boys are walking out. The whining of waifs, the weeping of wives, the wailing of workers must wind down!

Wars, war games, warships, war hawks, warplanes, war chests, war cries, warlords, war crimes are will-o'-the wisps of your once wacky, willful, whimsical ways!

Womanizers, women are no longer weak wahines, warm wax wads to work at whim with wicked warped wills; willing wet nurses to your welfarized, wizened world.

The world will withstand your willy-nilly waywardnesses. The Walden Pond watchers of the world will weld and weave what is wornout and worm-eaten. The weary weasels of worshiping wealth, and worshiping world power, are wounded and wrecked. The wild ones are whipped. Washed up warrants are written for war criminals! Whoopee!

The world will not whimper into a white dwarf wasted by your warheads!

EXERCISE 29

[j] Sound

1. Recite each horizontal and vertical group three times, holding the bracketed sound for four seconds:

[j]ah	[j]ay	[j]ee	[j]oo
[j]ay	[j]ee	[j]oo	[j]ah
[j]ee	[j]oo	[j]ah	[j]ay
[j]oo	[j]ah	[j]ay	[j]ee

CHART 8-4. The IPA Consonant Glide [j].

IPA Symbol	Sample	Type	Tongue	Lips or Mouth	Vocal Cords
j	*y*oung	voiced glide	tip behind lower front teeth, back raised higher toward hard palate than for [w], blade touching hard palate on each side, tongue ready to glide into position for following vowel	nearly closed, lips slightly drawn back, change position for following vowel	vibrating

2. Pronounce the following words containing [j], holding the [j] for four seconds:

Initial	Medial	Final
*y*elp	bull*i*on	No words end with this sound.
*y*east	al*i*en	
*y*awn	vermill*i*on	
*y*et	compan*i*on	
*y*ea	opin*i*on	
*y*ap	pavil*i*on	

3. Although many persons pronounce words like *student, duty, duke, tune, assume, Tuesday* with the vowel sound of *food, moon, fool,* the preferred pronunciation is still the vowel sound of *cube, pure,* and *human,* which is expressed in phonetics by [j] in combination with a vowel—[ju]. Read aloud the following pairs of words:

win you	western values
music student	beautiful wing

eastern yeast   Tuesday's views
feudal wooing   wet yacht
valiant stallion   wan yawn
familiar year   vermillion flower
well yelled   wild youth
walled yawl   alien wind

4. Match each word below with its correct phonetic counter-
    part. Sound each pair.

1. yacht _____ jɛlo
2. yoga _____ jɪr
3. you _____ jʌŋɪʃ
4. yam _____ jarn
5. yellow _____ jɛs
6. year _____ jahu
7. youngish _____ jæm
8. yarn _____ ju
9. yes _____ jat
10. Yahoo _____ joga

5. Recite as quickly as possible with accuracy:

        Yolanda, a yellow young yak,
        Yearned for a Yoga to whack;
        She yielded her yen to a young Jungian
        Whose fee was a yoke on the yak.

6. Look up the following words in your hardcovered diction-
    ary. Next to each word write its diacritical equivalent and
    the first definition given. All words will be found in the
    reading assigned.

	DIACRITICS	DEFINITIONS
yesteryear	_____	_____
quadrillion	_____	_____
Yosemite	_____	_____
yaks	_____	_____

yodelers	_____	_____
yew trees	_____	_____
Yucatan	_____	_____
Jungian	_____	_____
yawl	_____	_____
Yangtze	_____	_____
youngberry	_____	_____
Yerevan	_____	_____
Yahoos	_____	_____
yashmaks	_____	_____
vermillion	_____	_____

7. Read the following slowly for accuracy. In subsequent readings, try for interpretation and expression.

Yesteryear a quadrillion Sicilian Italians yielded to the yowling of yoga enthusiasts and held a yelling, yakity-yaking congenial Yo-Yo and billiard tournament for millions of yearning youths in beautiful Yosemite where yaks were ridden by Yankee yodelers. Beneath yellowing yew trees from Yucatan, Jungian Yugoslavians were eating yeasty yogurt mixed with onions and scallions. The reunion was consumed in fumes.

Nearby in the Yangtze River yachtsmen yawling in yawls and yachts yanked yolks of eggs and yellow pages from youngberry bushes.

From a youth hostel yattering came younglings from Yonkers, Yokahama, Yerevan, Yorktown, Yukon and Yumen. Yahoos, wearing yashmaks over vermillion limbs, served yummy yams and lighted yule logs.

COMBINATIONS

IPA consonant combinations join two IPA consonant sounds, specifically, a *plosive* followed by a *fricative*. There are two basic IPA consonant combinations: the *voiced* [dʒ] and the *voiceless* [tʃ].

CHART 8-5. The IPA Consonant Combination Sounds [dʒ] [tʃ]

IPA Symbol	Sample	Type	Tongue	Lips or Mouth	Vocal Cords
dʒ	*j*ust	voiced combination	blade to gum ridge behind upper teeth, sides of tongue against upper rear teeth blocking air for plosive, moving to fricative position	mouth slightly open, lips neutral on first sound, slightly protruding on second	vibrating
tʃ	*ch*in	unvoiced combination			non-vibrating

EXERCISE 30
[dʒ] *and* [tʃ] *Sounds*

Since the [ʃ] bears the same relationship to the [ʒ] sounds as the [t] does to the [d], being produced identically except that the first is unvoiced and the second voiced, the [tʃ] and the [dʒ] are also produced identically except that the first is unvoiced and the second voiced.

1. Recite each horizontal and vertical group three times:

[dʒ]ah   [dʒ]ah   [dʒ]ah   [dʒ]ah
[tʃ]ah   [tʃ]ah   [tʃ]ah   [tʃ]ah
[dʒ]ah   [dʒ]ah   [dʒ]ah   [dʒ]ah
[tʃ]ah   [tʃ]ah   [tʃ]ah   [tʃ]ah

2. Slowly pronounce the following words containing [dʒ]:

Initial	Medial	Final
jeep	wages	fudge
gyp	cogent	ridge
jet	gadget	rage
jury	pudgy	merge
jazz	wedges	gorge
just	regent	allege

3. Slowly pronounce the following words containing [tʃ]:

Initial	Medial	Final
champ	wretched	peach
chimpanzee	richest	church
cherry	ketchup	witch
check	etching	speech
choose	touchy	poach
chick	itchy	reach

4. To feel the distinction between [dʒ] and [tʃ], read aloud the following pairs of words:

rich ridge	ginny chin
etched edge	smudged smirch
chilly judge	lurched urge
jasper chip	junked chunk
chimp's ridge	Cholmondelay's gem
cheap fudge	charred sludge
jowled chow	ketchup smudge
choked joke	children's grudge

5. Match each word below with its correct phonetic counterpart. Sound each pair.

1. jury _____ dʒækæs
2. joint _____ dʒʌmp
3. jam _____ dʒɚk
4. jute _____ dʒʌt
5. jackass _____ dʒʌdʒ

6. jump _____ dʒʌst
7. jerk _____ dʒut
8. jut _____ dʒuri
9. just _____ dʒɔɪnt
10. judge _____ dʒæm

6. Look up the following words in your hardcovered dictionary. Next to each word write its diacritical equivalent and
the first definition given. All these words appear in the assigned reading.

	DIACRITICS	DEFINITIONS
Tchaikovsky		
Chekhov		
leechy		
chimerical		
beige		
chaise longue		
magenta		
chamois		
cadgers		
Cherokees		
Chippewa		
Chippendale		
jubilation		

7. Read the following slowly for accuracy. In subsequent
readings, try for interpretation and expression.

Legions of magic partridges perched on ledges of richly
churned margarine and charmed a huge chamber of cul-
tured chimpanzees by chirping Tchaikovsky and chortling
Chekhov.

In leechy ditches villagers chopped chunks of chalk
and charcoal from bulges of natural architecture. In con-
junction with this chimerical chopping, on a beige chaise
longue, richly stitched with a magenta chamois, perjured

codgers fetchingly questioned a huge menagerie of cagey judges.

Cheated Cherokees and Chippewa chiefs chanted on Chippendale chairs while chewing on chestnuts. Chummy Christians chanted a charming jumble of choice jubilations.

9

IPA Frontal Vowels

The IPA vowels are divided into three kinds: *frontal, medial,* and *back* vowel sounds. Frontal vowels are formed by the tip of the tongue in the front of the mouth. Medial vowels are formed by the middle of the tongue in the middle of the mouth. Back vowels are formed by the back of the tongue in the rear of the mouth.

But before beginning an examination of the vowel sounds, it is recommended that you make a strenuous review of the lip exercise in Chapter Three (Exercise 9). While making the vowel sounds of the exercise, think of a musician placing his fingers on the strings of a guitar or violin—your tongue work must be comparably accurate.

The frontal vowels are: [i] [ɪ] [e] [ɛ] [æ.]

If you concentrate on your tongue as you recite the frontal vowels, you will see that between [i] and [æ] the tongue moves progressively from a very high position to a low one. Simultaneously, the mouth changes progressively from an almost closed position to a noticeably open one.

150

EXERCISE 31
Frontal Vowel Sounds

1. Watching your mouth, tongue, and lips in a mirror as much as possible, recite the following words containing the frontal vowels, holding the vowel sounds for four seconds.

eat

it

mate

met

at

2. Now sound the vowels alone, holding each one for four seconds:

ea(t)	[i]
i(t)	[ɪ]
(m)a(te)	*[e]
(m)e(t)	[ɛ]
a(t)	[æ]

Repeat each of the above sounds three times. If you suspect that you are not hitting the right note, refer to the key word. Get the feeling of how your tongue moves from the high, tense placement of [i] to the lower, relaxed placement of [æ] as it proceeds down the scale. Play this scale a few times; then after sounding the first note [i], jump down to the bottom note [æ]. Use a mirror and notice that your lips are almost together on the [i] sound, but are parted quite a bit on the [æ] sound.

You will learn that not all vowel sounds are equally difficult to master. If it were not for Romance language speaking foreign students, I would state that the first four frontal vowels present no problem at all, but for foreign language speaking students the first two vowels *can* be a problem. However, the

---

* Remember, (e) will be used in place of the diphthong (eɪ).

last frontal vowel is a challenge for almost *all* students in the northeastern part of the United States.

The confusion between the first two frontal vowels, [i] and [ɪ] will be studied below, and exercises for their correction given. The [æ] problem for students in the northeastern part of the United States is compounded by the fact that it involves both the lips and the tongue, and speech habits for vowel formation are very hard to change. Remember the image of language being like a stream, with the consonants the stepping stones that can be pressed down on, and the vowels the flowing water, elusive and hard to control. Keep that image in mind when you start to work on the vowel sounds and don't get discouraged when you can't achieve immediate control, or when you discover that after you thought you had a vowel sound where you wanted it to be, it wasn't there at all.

The vowel section will not, therefore, contain the same sort of exercises as the consonant sections. Since the problems are different, the exercises must be different. Instead of the repetition of the sound in the initial position, as found in the consonant exercises, words supplying degrees of difficulty will be provided for practice in the sections below. These word exercises will help you to get a grasp on the elusive vowels.

CHART 9-1. The IPA Frontal Vowel [i].

IPA Symbol	Sample	Type	Tongue	Lips or Mouth	Vocal Cords
i	*eat*	frontal vowel	tip behind bottom front teeth, center arched toward hard palate, sides touching upper teeth	lips pulled into a smile, mouth almost closed	vibrating

EXERCISE 32
[i] Frontal Vowel Sound

Remember in exercise work to exaggerate lip positions to strengthen the muscles. On each [i] sound below, pull your lips back all the way. Use a mirror to watch the contrast in your lips as you make the different sounds. Correct sluggish lips; make them move. In the vowel exercises do not hold the vowels for four seconds; it is the consonants, not the vowels, that you must learn to use as stepping stones to clarity.

1. Repeat ten times:

   r[i]   w[i]   m[i]   w[i]

2. Using your mirror to check for exaggerated lip movement, slowly pronounce the following words containing [i]:

Initial	Medial	Final
eve	discreet	tee
eke	complete	we
ego	via	tree
even	treat	three
eager	venial	plea
easy	realist	see

3. Read aloud the following pairs of words:

three trees	deep dip
scheming Eve	weeping willow
cream cheese	bitter beet
fleet fleas	red reed
sweet pea	great glee
queen bee	keening wind
deep meaning	foundered fleet
preacher Beecher	reading room

4. Match each word below with its correct phonetic counterpart. Sound each pair.

1. heath _____ sið   6. reek _____ lif
2. trio _____ rik   7. seethe _____ lik
3. sheik _____ hiθ   8. wreath _____ jild
4. leaf _____ spik   9. yield _____ riθ
5. speak _____ ʃik   10. leak _____ trio

5. The difficulty in differentiating between [i] and [ɪ] arises from their proximity. Precise tongue placement is absolutely necessary and a hit or miss attitude will keep you in a state of utter confusion.

   Say the following, first making sure to pronounce the isolated vowels accurately.

[i]	[ɪ]	eat	it
[i]	[ɪ]	feet	fit
[i]	[ɪ]	meet	mit
[i]	[ɪ]	fleet	flit
[i]	[ɪ]	jeep	gyp
[ɪ]	[i]	it	eat
[ɪ]	[i]	fit	feet
[ɪ]	[i]	mit	meet
[ɪ]	[i]	flit	fleet
[ɪ]	[i]	gyp	jeep

1. "Cheep, cheep," peeped the pretty chick.
2. The green jeep was cheap, the gyp screeched.
3. Keep feet fit and feel fit.
4. Bits of meat and bits of beets are bitter.
5. Keep sheep in deep dips.
6. He slit the sleazy sheets in strips.
7. Sleeping beauty bit bits of sweet treats.
8. She and he sit in the heat hip to hip.
9. He bit, she bit, peach pits with teeth tips.
10. Leaves litter neat little streets.

6.   Recite as quickly as possible with accuracy:

> Over the ripening peach
> Buzzes the bee.
> Splash on the billowy beach
> Tumbles the sea.
> But the peach
> And the beach
> They are each
> Nothing to me!
>
> —W. S. GILBERT
> *Ruddigore*

> There was an Old Person of Chili,
> Whose conduct was painful and silly,
> He sat on the stairs, eating apples and pears,
> That imprudent Old Person of Chili.
>
> —EDWARD LEAR
> *The Complete Nonsense*

EXERCISE 33

[ɪ] *Frontal Vowel Sound*

CHART 9-2. The IPA Frontal Vowel [ɪ].

IPA Symbol	Sample	Type	Tongue	Lips or Mouth	Vocal Cords
ɪ	*it*	frontal vowel	tip behind bottom front teeth slightly lower than for [i], sides of tongue touching upper side teeth	lips very slightly drawn back, not so far as for [i], mouth slightly more open than for [i]	vibrating

1. Using your mirror to watch the contrast in exaggerated lip positions, repeat ten times:

r[ɪ]   w[ɪ]   m[ɪ]   w[ɪ]

2. Slowly pronounce the following words containing [ɪ]:

Initial	Medial	Final
inhale	implicit	In some regions the final [ɪ]
innate	kick	sound in words like *baby*,
initial	inordinate	*cookie, cherry* is pronounced
issue	inherit	[ɪ]. The [ɪ] sound is not recom-
itch	thin	mended, however.
ignominious	pill	

3. Read aloud the following pairs of words:

spinning disk	ditto machine
spitted pig	calculated risk
grisly grins	Scotch mist
thin vinegar	legal gyp
mixed biscuits	brisk walk
big city	quick tiger
twin sister	vivid shadows
pitiful kid	glimmering wheels

4. Match each word below with its correct phonetic counterpart. Sound each pair.

1. his _____ ʃɪp
2. chill _____ hɪs
3. hither _____ tɪnt
4. ship _____ ʃɪm
5. trip _____ trɪk

6. hiss _____ 'hɪðɚ
7. tint _____ dʒɪlt
8. jilt _____ trɪp
9. shim _____ hɪz
10. trick _____ tʃɪl

5. Read aloud the following sentences:

1. The wit had a fit when a nitwit made a quip that hit him on the quick.

2. On a chilly hill, Millie and Tillie had a still, where Bill and Will came to swill.
3. Whims can become habits, then sins difficult to kick.
4. If you itch, grip your fist, flip your wrist, and it will desist.
5. In the mist the grim twins swim amidst the thin, swift fins.
6. The skit is silly, skimpy, sinister and it stinks.
7. Six single, skinny Sing-Sing singers stimulated the skid row sickies in the sinkhole.
8. Interlinear links intensify the input instantly.
9. The insane insubordinate was installed in the institute.
10. The insects are insensitive to the insecticides which they inhale instinctively.

6. Recite as quickly as possible with accuracy:

> Here's a man of jollity,
> Jibe, joke, jollify!
> Give us of your quality,
> Come, fool, follify!
>
> If you vapour vapidly,
> River runneth rapidly,
> Into it we fling
> Bird who doesn't sing!
>
> Give us an experiment
> In the art of merriment;
> Into it we throw
> Cock who doesn't crow!
>
> Banish your timidity
> And with all rapidity
> Give us quip and quiddity—
> Willy-nilly, O!

—W. S. GILBERT
The Yeomen of the Guard

There was an Old Man on a hill,
Who seldom, if ever, stood still;
He ran up and down, in his Grandmother's gown,
Which adorned that Old Man on a hill.

—EDWARD LEAR
The Complete Nonsense

CHART 9-3. The IPA Frontal Vowel [e]. *

IPA Symbol	Sample	Type	Tongue	Lips or Mouth	Vocal Cords
e	lo'cate	frontal vowel, un-stressed syllable	tip behind bottom front teeth, tongue less high than for [ɪ], sides touching upper side teeth	lips drawn back less than for [ɪ], mouth more open	vibrating

EXERCISE 34
The [e] Frontal Vowel Sound

1. Using your mirror to watch the contrast in exaggerated lip positions, repeat ten times:

    r[e]   w[i]   m[e]   w[i]

2. Slowly pronounce the following words containing [e]:

    Initial   *Medial*   *Final*

    aid   nape   sleigh
    apex   made   tray

---

*See phonetic chart, p. 69 for explanation about [e] and [eɪ]. [eɪ] will be discussed as a diphthong in Chapter Eleven.

ailment	mail	nay
ale	sail	display
alias	name	today
alien	tame	fray

3. Read aloud the following pairs of words containing [e]:

fail safe	anchors aweigh
tame ape	wailing wall
veiled Asian	fearful ailment
late mail	neighing steed
frail male	hay ride
jail bait	honest Abe
sailing mate	full tray
flaming face	hairy ape

4. Match each word below with its correct phonetic counterpart. Sound each pair.

1. mate _____ mek
2. fate _____ sped
3. maid _____ tred
4. make _____ ren
5. rake _____ ven

6. spade _____ wed
7. trade _____ rek
8. wade _____ met
9. vain _____ med
10. rain _____ fet

5. Read aloud the following sentences:

1. He bet from his bed on the horse well bred.
2. The sled sped into the shed.
3. Ben was on the fen, yenning to pen his hen.
4. The wren flew over the egg again and again.
5. The best chessmen are generally not well read.
6. Hemingway did not help the effort.
7. Ted was held helpless in the massive melon.
8. Ed, Helen, Ned and Fred all said they would wed.
9. The devil is never going to lessen his effort to get you in hell.
10. This western epic will echo forever.

6. Repeat as rapidly as possible with accuracy:

> In a melancholy train,
> On and on I walk all day;
> Pity those who love in vain—
> None so sorrowful as they,
> Who can only sigh and say,
> Woe is me, alack a day!
>
> —W. S. GILBERT
> *Patience*

There was a Young Lady of Wales,
Who caught a large fish without scales;
When she lifted her hook, she exclaimed, 'Only look!'
That ecstatic Young Lady of Wales.

—EDWARD LEAR
The Complete Nonsense

CHART 9-4. The IPA Frontal Vowel [ɛ].

IPA Symbol	Sample	Type	Tongue	Lips or Mouth	Vocal Cords
ɛ	met	frontal vowel	tip behind bottom front teeth and tongue lower in mouth than for [e], sides of tongue touching upper teeth	mouth opened more than for [e] and lips neutral	vibrating

EXERCISE 35
The [ɛ] Frontal Vowel Sound

1. Using your mirror to watch the contrast in exaggerated lip positions, repeat ten times:

r[ɛ]   w[i]   m[ɛ]   w[i]

2. Slowly pronounce the following words containing [ɛ]:

Initial	*Medial*	*Final*
epic	tred	No words
elf	wed	end with
enter	bled	this sound.
egg	hedge	
effort	necklace	
echo	peccadillo	

3. Read aloud the following pairs of words:

clever epic	blood wedding
red devil	quelled mob
never better	rectified wrong
expensive retinue	ghastly spectre
Edward Confessor	steaming vegetable
market speculator	preached repentance
whetted appetite	dewy nectar
precious letter	clear spectrum

4. Match each word below with its correct phonetic counter-
    part. Sound each pair.

1. pet _____ bɛd
2. jealous _____ ʃɛf
3. hem _____ bidɛk
4. check _____ hɛnpɛk
5. bed _____ tʃɛs

6. chef _____ hɛm
7. bell _____ 'dʒɛləs
8. bedeck _____ bɛl
9. henpeck _____ tʃɛk
10. chess _____ pɛt

5. Read aloud the following sentences:

1. The rain in Spain falls mainly in the plain.
2. The date of the maid with the hairy ape was not top
    rate.
3. The reign of the train was in vain against the coming
    of the airplane.
4. They raked the apricots with a spade.

5. In Jamaica they bake hay under a hot sun's rays.
6. They say a tray on the way will make the day.
7. Say, Ray, pray, pay the maid.
8. A gay display saved the May Day.
9. Rachel raved about the raid during the earthquake.
10. Rafael, the radiologist, waded about the range waist deep in raisins.

6. Recite as quickly as possible with accuracy:

Freddie the frog would wed;
He needed a frog in his bed.
Every froggie said 'No!'
Every froggie said 'Go!'
So Fred wed a tadpole instead.

There was an Old Man of Kilkenny,
Who never had more than a penny;
He spent all that money, in onions and honey,
That wayward Old Man of Kilkenny.

—EDWARD LEAR
The Complete Nonsense

CHART 9-5. The IPA Frontal Vowel [æ].

IPA Symbol	Sample	Type	Tongue	Lips or Mouth	Vocal Cords
[æ]	sat	frontal vowel	tip behind bottom front teeth, tongue arched very slightly, no contact with upper teeth	mouth open wider than for [ɛ], lips neutral	vibrating

EXERCISE 36

The [æ] *Frontal Vowel Sound*

The [æ] phoneme is the only frontal vowel that presents regular difficulty to students. It is particularly difficult for Americans from the northeastern states. The main reason for the trouble is the failure of speakers from this region to open their mouths wide enough and to keep their tongues low in their mouths. Perhaps tension keeps the jaw tight and closed so as to flatten the roundness of the vowel. A tight mouth, of course, harms the efficiency of the mouth as a megaphone and also causes an unpleasant nasality.

In the exercises below, try to get the feel of the sound as it rolls off your tongue, and you will quickly advance beyond students who try to rely on their ears to get at this elusive sound. You must find the exact placement for the lip and for the tongue muscles.

1. Using your mirror to watch the contrast in exaggerated lip and mouth positions, repeat four times:

    r[æ]   w[i]   m[æ]   w[i]

    Concentrate on the feel of the difference between [i] and [æ]. Here is the difference: [i] requires a high tongue and a nearly closed mouth, whereas [æ] requires a low tongue and an open mouth. Once your muscles capture these feelings, they won't let you down.

2. This exercise may be easy for you; it is meant to be. Get the *feel* of the phoneme [æ] by *chanting* each sound.

    sat-sat-sat-sat-sat-sat-sat-sat
    hat-hat-hat-hat-hat-hat-hat-hat
    fat-fat-fat-fat-fat-fat-fat-fat
    tat-tat-tat-tat-tat-tat-tat-tat
    ask-ask-ask-ask-ask-ask-ask-ask
    at-at-at-at-at-at-at-at-at-at
    bat-bat-bat-bat-bat-bat-bat-bat

3. The next set of words is more difficult. It contains consonants that require lip and tongue positions that are just the opposite of the lip and tongue positions required for the [æ] sound. You will have to move from the closed mouth and high tongue position of the [s] phoneme, for instance, to the open mouth and low tongue of the [æ] phoneme.

How can you tell if you are correct when you are at home alone? You can use a tape recorder. Or you can use the Chanting Exercise (see page 217) to hear yourself, or you can simply hold your nose, which will tell you whether you have blocked your mouth with either your tongue or your lips. Remember, your mouth is an efficient megaphone if not blocked. If, when you hold your nose, you feel a strong vibration, then you will know that you have flattened the [æ] vowel and made it nasal. When in doubt, hold your snout.

4. Pronounce each word three times: then chant each word carefully.

galaxy	half	lamp	stand	trance
salad	mallet	hand	diagram	manic
sandman	grass	mango	plaid	gangster
lamb	scram	telegram	prance	glance
mask	tank	grasp	plaster	glass
answer	band	dance	rash	clash
Sarah	manhood	mask	Sam	bombast

5. Read aloud the following sentences:

1. The gas tank blasted the clan of masked gangsters into the next galaxy.
2. The man asked the tramps not to dance on the grass.
3. The telegrams, bad and sad, were passed on to the staff.
4. Clams from the bland sand were grand.
5. Sam, Pam and Nan ran to get tan.

6. The bombastic master held the masses in manic trances.
7. Nabbing his last chance, the frantic wag grabbed the candied apple.
8. You can't cram for an oral speech exam.
9. They ate hash behind the glass because they had a rash.
10. The mass was held on the grass, under brass gas lamps with added glass.

6. Slowly pronounce the following words containing [æ]:

Initial	*Medial*	*Final*
astral	sham	No words
agnostic	cram	end with
avaricious	program	this sound.
avenue	frantic	
azure	wag	
avid	pasture	

7. Read aloud the following pairs of words:

grand tally	drag strip
ragamuffin rapscallions	candid camera
nasty taskmaster	sweet charity
avaricious scavenger	waxen beauty
vast expanses	last chance
candied apple	pastoral duty
grab bag	screeching bagpipe
bad habit	murderous dagger

8. Match each word below with its correct phonetic counterpart. Sound each pair.

1. tax	_____ ræpt		6. banner	_____ bændt	
2. tattler	_____ plæn		7. stagger	_____ tæks	
3. ranch	_____ ræðɚ		8. shag	_____ tætlɚ	
4. bandit	_____ bænɚ		9. plan	_____ræntʃ	
5. rapt	_____ ʃæg		10. rather	_____ 'stægɚ	

9.   Recite as quickly as possible with accuracy:

> Ghastly, ghastly!
> When man, sorrowful,
> Firstly, lastly,
> Of to-morrow full,
> After tarrying,
> Yields to harrying—
> Goes a-marrying.
> Ghastly, ghastly!
>
> —W. S. GILBERT
> *The Yeomen of the Guard*

There was an Old Man of Madras,
Who rode on a cream-coloured ass;
But the length of its ears, so promoted his fears,
That it killed that Old Man of Madras.

—EDWARD LEAR
The Complete Nonsense

10

IPA Medial and Back Vowels

MEDIAL VOWELS

The medial vowels are made with the middle of the tongue. The four important medial vowel sounds might actually be considered as two. However, each of the two basic sounds formed with the middle of the tongue changes enough between its occurrence in a stressed and an unstressed syllable to be designated by different phonetic syllables. It is therefore considered that there are at least four medial vowel sounds.

There is a possible fifth medial vowel sound for which the phonetic symbol [ɜ] is used. This is the sound used in *bird* by some persons in the eastern and southern United States where the *r* is dropped. However, as this book is covering General American Speech, no practice exercises are provided. The IPA medial vowels discussed in this chapter are the following: [ɝ] [ɚ] [ʌ] [ə]

EXERCISE 37
IPA Medial Vowel Sounds

The difficult phoneme in this group is the [ɝ] phoneme, which is defined as a medial vowel with an [r] coloring. The [r] coloring is indicated by the small hook at the top of the symbol. Americans from the coastal regions of Maine, New York City, and Georgia tend to omit the [r] coloring, though the famous tendency of Brooklynites to say *boid* is lessening.

The difficulty in pronouncing the [ɝ] phoneme is caused by the tongue placement it requires. It is made by raising the middle of the tongue fairly high in the mouth. Just as the difficulty with the frontal vowel [æ] occurs because the tongue is up when it should be down, the difficulty with the medial vowel [ɝ] occurs because the tongue is down when it should be up. Of course the same problem develops in dealing with the semivowel [r].

Like frontals, the medial vowels can also be "played" like a scale, the tongue lowering itself in the mouth and the mouth opening increasing.

1. Watching your mouth, tongue, and lips in a mirror as closely as possible, recite the following words containing the medial vowels, holding the vowel sounds for four seconds:

> b*ir*d   (stressed)
> ev*er*   (unstressed)
> c*u*t   (stressed)
> *a*bove   (unstressed)

2. Now voice the vowel sounds alone, holding each one for four seconds:

> (b)*ir*(d) . . . . [ɝ] stressed
> (ev)*er* . . . . [ɚ] unstressed
> (c)*u*(t) . . . . [ʌ] stressed
> *a*(bove) . . . . [ə] unstressed

EXERCISE 38
[ɝ] *and* [ɚ] *Medial Vowel Sounds*

Of this group [ɝ] is the same sound as [ɚ], but the first occurs in stressed syllables and the second in unstressed syllables.

CHART 10-1. The IPA Medial Vowels [ɝ] and [ɚ].

IPA Symbol	Sample	Type	Tongue	Lips or Mouth	Vocal Cords
ɝ	bird	medial vowel, stressed syllable	sides of tongue pressed firmly against upper rear molars, tip free	lips firm, mouth almost closed	vibrating
ɚ	ever	medial vowel, un-stressed syllable			

1. Slowly pronounce the following words which contain the stressed [ɝ]:

Initial	Medial	Final
urn	surge	cur
earth	pert	her
irksome	verdict	aver
earning	surf	prefer
erst	nerve	whir
urban	hurt	concur

2. Slowly pronounce the following words which contain the unstressed [ɚ]:

sister	mother	ever
under	meager	bother
fatter	skater	neuter
pewter	player	better
brother	father	later
larger	stronger	homer
thinner	worker	other
rocker	doer	longer

3. Match each word below, containing the phoneme [ɝ], with its correct phonetic counterpart. Sound each pair.

1. third _____ mɝ·si
2. term _____ 'mɝ·dɚ
3. swerve _____ θɝ·d
4. mercy _____ də'vɝ·s
5. nerve _____ sɝ·tə‚faɪ

6. murder _____ tɝ·m
7. diverse _____ bɝ·θ
8. certify _____ nɝ·v
9. berth _____ tɝ·maɪt
10. termite _____ swɝ·v

4. Match each word below, containing the phoneme [ɚ] with its correct phonetic counterpart. Sound each pair.

1. sister _____ 'ɛvɚ
2. cider _____ 'niðɚ
3. speaker _____ 'klɛvɚ
4. ledger _____ 'wɝ·kɚ
5. ever _____ 'mʌðɚ

6. neither _____ 'sistɚ
7. worker _____ 'spikɚ
8. mother _____ 'maɪzɚ
9. miser _____ 'lɛdʒɚ
10. clever _____ 'saɪdɚ

5. Read the following sentences and get the feeling of the differences between the unstressed [ɚ] and the stressed [ɝ].

1. He said he never heard the third bird.
2. It is better to yearn and learn than to yearn and spurn learning.
3. The mercenaries surveyed the terminal from a perch on the porch.
4. New Yorkers are in terror of litter and bitter vapors.
5. The tutor was jocular when he was paid *per diem* but morose when he was remunerated yearly.
6. The sterling silver stirrup was removed by a master of legerdemain.
7. The nurse was from New Jersey but articulated like a New Yorker.
8. The martyr had to order a permit in order to burn and churn in a gyre.
9. The jocular lady-killer was layered in leather and heather in the hotter weather.
10. The master of verbiage was over the hearse but his verse was mercifully terse.

6.   Recite as quickly as possible with accuracy:

> There was an Old Lady of Chertsey,
> Who made a remarkable curtsey;
> She twirled round and round, till she sunk underground,
> Which distressed all the people of Chertsey.

—EDWARD LEAR
The Complete Nonsense

EXERCISE 39
[ʌ] *and* [ə] *Medial Vowel Sounds*

Of this group, [ʌ] is the same sound as [ə], but the first occurs in stressed syllables and the second in unstressed syllables.
The [ə] is also called the *schwa*, a neutral-sounding vowel that
always occurs in unaccented syllables and towards which the
vowel sounds in unaccented syllables always tend. It is the most
common vowel sound in English.

The versatile schwa bears the same relationship to [ɜ]—the
r-less pronunciation of the vowel sound in *bird*—that it does to
[ʌ]. In the parts of the East and South where the r is dropped,
when the [ɜ] occurs in an unaccented syllable it becomes the
schwa, as in *ever*, pronounced without the final r. The pronunciation of the r is recommended for General American Speech,
however, with the restriction of the schwa to the [ʌ] sound of
unaccented syllables.

CHART 10-2. IPA Medial Vowels [ə] and [ʌ].

IPA Symbol	Sample	Type	Tongue	Lips or Mouth	Vocal Cords
ʌ	cut	medial vowel, stressed syllable	tip behind bottom teeth, middle raised toward hard palate	lips neutral, mouth slightly open	vibrating
ə	above	medial vowel, un-stressed syllable			

1. Using your mirror to watch the contrast in exaggerated lip positions, repeat ten times:

   r[ʌ]   w[i]   m[ʌ]   w[i]

2. Slowly pronounce the following words containing [ʌ]:

Initial	Medial	Final
udder	summer	No words
ultimate	ruff	end with
ulcer	fuss	this sound.
utter	humble	
under	vulture	
usher	sunder	

3. Read aloud the following pairs of words containing [ʌ]:

tungsten bulb	soothing lullaby
rushing bus	ugly tyke
dumb luck	undulating tentacle
humble nun	neat cut
knuckle under	hot lunch
shunned onion	humid summer
lustrous sun	screaming vulture
honey bun	such nerve

4. Slowly pronounce the following words containing [ə], remembering to keep the syllable containing it unaccented:

Initial	Medial	Final
afar	unaffected	Sierra
affix	vernal	Dakota
astrology	vassalage	tuba
appeal	Saracen	pizza
aloof	alphabet	scrofula
aloft	syllable	iota

5. Match each word below, containing the phoneme [ʌ], with its correct phonetic counterpart. Sound each pair.

1. spud _____ rʌn
2. club _____ trʌk
3. rug _____ θʌd
4. truck _____ hʌŋk
5. buzz _____ bʌtɚ

6. thud _____ spʌd
7. hunk _____ klʌb
8. butter _____ krʌst
9. run _____ bʌz
10. crust _____ rʌg

6. Match each word below, containing the phoneme [ə], with its correct phonetic counterpart. Sound each pair.

7. Read aloud the following sentences:

   1. The ugly bum ate his buns with the nuns.
   2. "Alone, alone, all, all alone!" said the bug in the rug.
   3. Cut the pizza in the hut beyond the rut.
   4. The tuba player hunted around for a hundred humble Huns.
   5. The humid summer hushed the cruddy city's hum.
   6. The trucker plunked the hunk of buttered bananas with a thud.
   7. About one o'clock the mugger hugged the crusty mutt by mistake.
   8. "Hup! Hup! Hup!" the Marine sergeant buzzed aloud.
   9. Alone the mummy munched on club sandwiches of muddy pig's knuckles.
   10. The uncle, an underling, was utterly alone, yet aloof.

1. method _____ əlaud
2. banana _____ ə'klɑk
3. attest _____ əlon
4. about _____ əplaɪ
5. circa _____ mɛθəd

6. apply _____ bə'nænə
7. around _____ ə'tɛst
8. aloud _____ əbaut
9. alone _____ 'sɝ·kə
10. o'clock _____ əraund

8. Recite as quickly as possible with accuracy:

> There was an old mutt in a rut
> Who fell in and out of his hut;
> "I'll yell and I'll shout 'till they come pull me out,"
> Said the mutt in the rut by the hut.

BACK VOWELS

The back vowels are a range of vowels formed by movement of the back of the tongue. As you proceed through the range, the back of the tongue lowers and the mouth opening grows larger. Back vowels consist of the following group: [u] [ʊ] [o*] [ɔ] [a]

The first back vowel uses a tense, puckered, lip position contrasted to the wide open, relaxed mouth position for the last vowel. Try going from [u] (oooo) to a wide [a] (ahhh: the sound a doctor asks for when he wants to see into the mouth).

CHART 10-3. The IPA Back Vowel [u].

IPA Symbol	Sample	Type	Tongue	Lips or Mouth	Vocal Cords
u	moon	back vowel	tip behind bottom front teeth, back raised near soft palate	mouth rounded with small opening, lips slightly protruded	vibrating

---

* See the index for further information concerning [o] and the diphthong [oʊ].

EXERCISE 40
[u] *Back Vowel Sound*

1. Watching your mouth, tongue, and lips in a mirror as much as possible, recite the following words containing the back vowels, holding the vowel sounds for four seconds:

    > m*oo*n
    > t*oo*k
    > *o*bey
    > *a*we
    > f*a*ther

2. Now form the vowel sounds alone, holding each one for four seconds:

(m)*oo*(n)	[u]
(t)*oo*(k)	[ʊ]
o(bey)	[o]
*a*w(e)	[ɔ]
(f)*a*(ther)	[ɑ]

[u] is a delicate sound with two phonemic relations: [ʊ] as in *took* and [ʌ] as in *cut*. Historically [ʊ] developed as a relaxed form of [u], and then later [ʌ] developed as a relaxed form of [ʊ]. This is why words spelled with the letters *u*, *oo*, and *o* are all related to the three phonemes, and it accounts for the difficulty foreign speakers have with the *oo* in *moon*, which is [u] and the *oo* in *book*, which is [ʊ].

[u] is also delicate because it comes from a tense lip placement, with rounded lips puckered as for a kiss, and a tongue that is tense with the back high and raised. You can understand why common usage would want to relax that demanding sound.

EXERCISE 41
[u] *Back Vowel Sound*

In common usage words like *duty, duke, assume,* become flattened, losing the crisp delicacy of the [u]. The flattening is caused by the relaxation of the lips from the forward position, and the lowering of the back of the tongue; it is a matter of laziness. Take the word *puke:* it contains the [u] but anyone can sound the [u] in it with all the necessary precision. This is because the plosive [p] puts the lips automatically into the puckered forward position, and raises the tongue in perfect preparation for the [u] correctly pronounced. Try the same sound, now, in some more difficult positions.

1. Using your mirror to watch the contrast in exaggerated lip positions, repeat ten times:

    r[u]   w[i]   m[u]   w[i]

2. Slowly pronounce the following words containing [u]:

Initial	Medial	Final
No words begin with this sound.	moose	hue
	troop	true
	loot	zoo
	brood	screw
	cute	through
	loom	tattoo

3. Read aloud the following pairs of words containing [u]:

true voodoo	cream soup
loose caboose	queen's fool
foolish kangaroo	rude wood
wounded crew	leaking roof
true blue	bugled tattoo
blue moon	sneaking snoop

school shoes   choking croup
cool crew   melodious lute

4. Match each word below with its correct phonetic counter-part. Sound each pair.

1. assume _____ brud
2. doom _____ gun
3. bruise _____ glu
4. peruse _____ brut
5. brood _____ bruz

6. choose _____ dum
7. goon _____ frut
8. glue _____ tʃuz
9. brute _____ pəˈruz
10. fruit _____ əˈsum

5. Read the following sentences for the [u] sound. Take particular care with lip placement.

1. Every Tuesday the duke assumed it was his duty to puke.
2. Every noon we choose to loosen the balloons.
3. Tools in June are needed in the blooming garden.
4. The prudent man avoids ruin.
5. I assume that you will resume your duties.
6. The loony Boone would shoot at the chewed up spoons.
7. Chooscy Ruth tells the truth and nothing but the truth.
8. Goodie Two Shoes is too good to be true.
9. Do is doing but ruing is doing nothing but stewing.
10. The fruits come by canoe with two recruits who toot flutes.

Recite as quickly as possible with accuracy:

There was a young lady in blue,
Who said, 'Is it you? Is it you?'
When they said, 'Yes, it is,'—She replied only, 'Whizz!'
That ungracious young lady in blue.

—EDWARD LEAR
The Complete Nonsense

A kangaroo with the flu
Rued that he flew like a gnu;
So he stiffened his tail with glue from a pail
And the flu flew the glued kangaroo.

CHART 10-4. The IPA Back Vowel [ʊ].

IPA Symbol	Sample	Type	Tongue	Lips or Mouth	Vocal Cords
ʊ	took	back vowel	tip behind bottom front teeth, back lower than for [u]	lips less rounded than for [u], more nearly neutral, mouth more open	vibrating

EXERCISE 42
[ʊ] *Back Vowel Sound*

1. Using your mirror to watch the contrast in exaggerated lip positions, repeat ten times:

r[ʊ]   w[i]   m[ʊ]   w[i]

2. Slowly pronounce the following words containing [ʊ]:

Initial	Medial	Final
No words begin with this sound.	soot book could wood put look	No words end with this sound.

3. Read aloud the following pair of words containing [ʊ]:

good woman	bully beef
full brook	shook fist
could cook	crude wood
bushy woods	speech book
bull's foot	wool ball
hoody crook	stood still
cooked pudding	cute looking
sooty rook	love nook

4. Match each word below with its correct phonetic counterpart. Sound each pair.

1. book _____ gʊd
2. shook _____ wʊd
3. hood _____ kʊd
4. good _____ lʊk
5. rook _____ hʊk

6. wood _____ bʊk
7. could _____ hʊd
8. look _____ rʊk
9. should _____ ʃʊd
10. hook _____ ʃʊk

5. Read aloud the following sentences:

1. Sugar from Sumatra is sure to make one smug.
2. The cook would not look at the bull.
3. The hook in the brook was forsook.
4. He shook in his hood all he could.
5. Don't pussyfoot, put the soot on the pulley.
6. The pushcart men all pushed the pullman car.
7. Pushkin, a purist, played a putative game of pushball.
8. The man mauled the mural with muriatic acid.
9. He withstood the tourniquet as best he could.
10. Would that I could what I should!

6. Recite as quickly as possible with accuracy:

Butch the rook,
By his friends forsook,
Was hooked by a book
In a nook by a brook;
Now the rook's by the brook with the book if you look.

CHART 10-5. The IPA Back Vowel [o].

IPA Symbol	Sample	Type	Tongue	Lips or Mouth	Vocal Cords
o	*obey*	back vowel	tip behind bottom front teeth, back lower than for [ʊ]	lips rounded with slight tension, mouth more open than for [ʊ]	vibrating

EXERCISE 43
[o] *Back Vowel Sound*

As noted earlier, there was a time when phoneticians considered the [o] sound to exist only in unstressed syllables. When it occurred in the stressed syllable, it was considered to be the diphthong [oʊ]. However, almost all phoneticians now concur that the distinction between the two sounds is so difficult to make that they are virtually indistinguishable. For this reason we shall use the phoneme [o] in both stressed and unstressed syllables to indicate the sound, and the diphthong [oʊ] will not be studied among the diphthongs.

1. Using your mirror to watch the contrast in exaggerated lip positions, repeat ten times:

    r[o]   w[i]   m[o]   w[i]

2. Slowly pronounce the following words which contain [o]:

Initial	Medial	Final
odor	moat	blow
ogle	roast	below
oath	load	know
oasis	bone	so
omen	home	though
odious	lope	throw

3. Read aloud the following pairs of words containing [o]:

loathsome crow	Grecian ode
broken stone	sour dough
smoking stove	hemp rope
slow motion	sharp slope
oval loaf	warty toad
flowing bowl	loan shark
woeful moan	sewn seam
hoed row	whoa boy

4. Match each word below with its correct phonetic counterpart. Sound each pair.

1. vote _____ ʃon		6. show _____ rot	
2. boat _____ dot		7. row _____ blot	
3. dote _____ rot		8. rote _____ vot	
4. quota _____ bot		9. wrote _____ ʃo	
5. shown _____ ro		10. bloat _____ 'kwotə	

5. Read aloud the following sentences:

1. The queen toad was rowed in a boat by the toad rowers.
2. The code showed that it was owed to Olympus.
3. The moat was filled with odorous okra.
4. "Dote on the quote I wrote!" opined the opium eater.
5. Show me the oboe; then let me know when to blow it.
6. Okeechobee is not in Okinawa or Omaha.
7. "O solo mio" is not an ode to a doe.
8. The Okies of Oklahoma were openfaced, openhearted and openhanded.
9. "Heigh ho, heigh ho, Snow White we love you so!"
10. The opus to Oberon was overwhelming.

6. Recite as quickly as possible with accuracy:

There was an Old Man in a boat,
Who said, 'I'm afloat! I'm afloat!'

When they said, 'No! you ain't!' he was ready to faint,
That unhappy Old Man in a boat.

—EDWARD LEAR
The Complete Nonsense

A toad wrote an ode to a crow,
Scorned, he told his woe:
'Oh, crow, you must own that your heart is as stone,
So my next ode will go to a doe.'

CHART 10-6. The IPA Back Vowel [ɔ].

IPA Symbol	Sample	Type	Tongue	Lips or Mouth	Vocal Cords
ɔ	*awe*	back vowel	tip behind bottom front teeth, back lower than for [o]	lips rounded, mouth more open than for [o]	vibrating

EXERCISE 44
[ɔ] *Back Vowel Sound*

In pronouncing the [ɔ] be careful not to let the lips protrude forward into a [w] position, and keep the mouth opened quite wide. Keep lips rounded and relaxed, tongue down.

A regional variation of this sound occurs in the northeastern parts of our country. Just as the [æ] phoneme is flattened by a closed mouth and a high tongue position, so the [ɔ] phoneme is flattened in the same way into a nasal sound that is unpleasant to the listener. To avoid flattening such words as *on, lost, gone, all,* take care to keep the mouth open and avoid flattening and raising the tongue. If the tongue is very much flattened and raised, an intrusive *r* results and the word *law* will become *lore.* Or the [ɪ] phoneme may be added to the [ɔ] to form the diphthong [ɔɪ], in which case *gone* (gɔn) is distorted to gɔɪn, and *on* (ɔn) is distorted to ɔɪn.

1. Using your mirror to watch the contrast in exaggerated lip positions, repeat ten times:

    r[ɔ]   w[i]   m[ɔ]   w[i]

2. Slowly pronounce the following words which contain [ɔ]:

Initial	Medial	Final
auspice	mawkish	flaw
alder	brought	jaw
austere	laud	withdraw
awning	launch	paw
augury	raucous	law
always	fawn	seesaw

3. Read aloud the following pairs of words which contain [ɔ]:

odd law	cawing crew
squawking hawk	striped awning
lobster sauce	much sought
fall audit	long haul
awkward squaw	bitter gall
tall cop	old song
lost faucet	austere monk
bought shawl	spicy sauce

4. Match each word below with its correct phonetic counterpart. Sound each pair.

1. draw _____ 'mɔdlin
2. law _____ bɔrn
3. door _____ 'mɔkɪʃ
4. pour _____ drɔ
5. fork _____ lɔ

6. mawkish _____ fɔrm
7. born _____ dɔr
8. morn _____ pɔr
9. maudlin _____ fɔrk
10. form _____ mɔrn

5. Read aloud the following sentences:

   1. He thought he saw the fawn on the lawn.
   2. The law of the land is not the same as the lore of the land.

3. The Austrian autocrat talked of the auto-da-fé.
4. The hawk squawked on the stalk.
5. The audiophyle listened like an automaton.
6. The augury was augmented with awful small talk.
7. The automat held no aura for the auto sales force.
8. The aurora borealis was auspicious for all.
9. The authentic author authenticated the autobiography.
10. "Walk, don't talk, and be sure to balk it!"

6. Recite as quickly as possible with accuracy:

> A hawk and an auk in the ark
> Made a squawk and a squall in the dark;
> They said, 'If we're raucous and sound like a caucus,
> Can't a hawk and an auk have a lark?'
>
> A haughty young lady from Daughty
> Whose ideas were excessively naughty
> Climbed up a tree to examine the sea,
> The haughty, young lady of Daughty.

—EDWARD LEAR
The Complete Nonsense

CHART 10-7. The IPA Back Vowel [ɑ].

IPA Symbol	Sample	Type	Tongue	Lips or Mouth	Vocal Cords
[ɑ]	father	back vowel	tip behind bottom front teeth, back of tongue lower than for [ə]—this is the lowest tongue position for any sound made	mouth wide open, lips relaxed	vibrating

EXERCISE 45
[ɑ] *Back Vowel Sound*

1. Using your mirror to watch the contrast in exaggerated lip positions, repeat ten times:

r[ɑ]   w[i]   m[ɑ]   w[i]

2. Note that the General American Speech pronunciation for the initial sound in the word *operate* is [ɑ]. Slowly pronounce the following words which contain [ɑ]:

Initial	*Medial*	*Final*
are	nominee	spa
honest	noggin	ma
oblivion	calm	la
onset	balm	fa
art	cod	hurrah
archive	quad	shah

3. Read aloud the following pairs of words containing [ɑ]:

hard omnibus	reluctant nominee
hoorah Sam	thronged spa
startled swan	cheap onyx
odd rock	cheery noggin
dark palm	deep calm
lolling doll	odd object
darling llama	solemn psalm
darned sock	crowded quad

4. Match each word below with its correct phonetic counterpart. Sound each pair.

1. not _____ rɑk   3. spot _____ pɑp
2. rot _____ hɑt   4. rock _____ nɑt

5. atop _____ gɑt   8. got _____ pɑt,æʃ
6. hot _____ spɑt   9. what _____ ə'tɑp
7. pop _____ 'ʌɑt   10. potash _____ rɑt

5. Read aloud the following sentences:

  1. She wore her bonnet with a ribbon of angora on it.
  2. The mod squad met in the quad.
  3. The dogma was pronounced from the cupola.
  4. The calm lama was calmer than the farmer who had no karma.
  5. The duenna of La Mancha loved the viola cadenza.
  6. The nocturne was monochromatic.
  7. The racketeer met the rocketeer in the monastery.
  8. Some pots were terra-cotta; some were china.
  9. The nocturnal stigmatic danced the tarantella.
  10. At the cinema they served kasha and lox.

6. Recite as quickly as possible with accuracy:

> 'When tempests wreck thy bark,
> And all is drear and dark,
> If thou shouldst need an ark,
> I'll give thee one!'

> 'I heard the minx remark
> She'd meet him after dark
> Inside St. James's Park,
> And give him one!'
>
> —W. S. GILBERT
> *Iolanthe*

There was a Young Lady whose bonnet,
Came untied when the birds sate upon it;
But she said, 'I don't care! all the birds in the air
Are welcome to sit on my bonnet!'

—EDWARD LEAR
The Complete Nonsense

11

IPA Diphthongs

$\mathcal{D}$iphthongs are combinations of two vowel sounds that blend as if they were one. The stress is always on the first sound and never on the second. Diphthongs are spoken so quickly that it is virtually impossible to tell where one vowel sound ends and the other begins. In all diphthongs, the tongue moves from a low position for the first sound to a high position for the second sound. Another shared characteristic is that in all diphthongs the mouth opening moves from wider on the first sound to smaller on the second sound. The following IPA vowels are known as *diphthongs:* [eɪ*] [ɑɪ] [ɔɪ] [ɑʊ] [oʊ*]

---

* Although the diphthongs [eɪ] and [oʊ] are included here in the chart, they are, as I have said above, so difficult to distinguish from the single phonemes [e] and [o] that the sound is now usually transcribed by the use of the single phonemes.

The diphthongs are shown in their traditional sequence, but there will be no practice exercises for [eɪ] and [oʊ]. To practice these sounds, see the exercises for single phonemes [e] and [o].

EXERCISE 46
Diphthong Sounds

1. Repeat the following words, which contain diphthongs, and watch for the characteristics mentioned above:

ice   [aɪ]
oil   [ɔɪ]
cow   [aʊ]

CHART 11-1. The IPA Diphthong [aɪ].

IPA Symbol	Sample	Type	Tongue	Lips or Mouth	Vocal Cords
aɪ	*ice*	diph-thong	tip behind bottom front teeth, tongue low in bottom of mouth, middle of tongue arching toward hard palate for production of [ɪ]	open and relaxed for [a], closing for production of [ɪ]	vibrating

EXERCISE 47
[aɪ] *Sound*

1. Using your mirror to watch the contrast in exaggerated lip positions, repeat ten times:

r[aɪ]   w[i]   m[aɪ]   w[i]

2. Slowly pronounce the following words containing [aɪ]:

Initial	Medial	Final
icing	rice	my
idle	trice	try
ire	tried	spry
ivy	pride	high
eye	crime	fly
item	spite	bye

3. Read aloud the following pairs of words containing [aɪ]:

lime pie	heathen idol
high tide	crime wave
bicycle tire	dry dock
kite flying	nail file
dry ice	Captain Bligh
climbing ivy	middle aisle
ironic rhyme	biting tongue
why cry	nice point

4. Match each word below with its correct phonetic counterpart. Sound each pair.

1. thrice _____ twaɪs
2. mice _____ daɪs
3. spies _____ vaɪs
4. wise _____ naɪs
5. rise _____ laɪs

6. vice _____ θraɪs
7. twice _____ waɪs
8. nice _____ maɪs
9. dice _____ spaɪz
10. lice _____ raɪz

5. Read aloud the following sentences:

1. Thrice he threw the dice and thrice they turned into mice.
2. It is wise to rise early to avoid vice.
3. His eye beheld the sky.
4. In the dry pie sat the fly, and how it did cry.
5. Try to tie the spy to the kite for a spying flight.
6. Ice is nicer than fire, rhymed the poet.
7. Bligh sighed and then cried when the Bounty sailed by.

8. Some hike, some bike, but I personally would rather fly high in a glider.

9. The ivy is climbing, the crime wave is climbing, and the tide is climbing higher too.

10. "Goodbye," said the shy guy to his Siamese cat with the wide eyes.

6. Repeat as rapidly as possible with accuracy:

> If you're anxious for to shine in the high aesthetic line
> as a man of culture rare,
> You must get up all the germs of the transcendental
> terms, and plant them everywhere,
> You must lie upon the daisies, and discourse in novel
> phrases of your complicated state of mind,
> The meaning doesn't matter if it's only idle chatter
> of a transcendental kind.

—W. S. GILBERT
Patience

> There was an Old Man of the Isles,
> Whose face was pervaded with smiles:
> He sung high dum diddle, and played on the fiddle,
> That amiable Man of the Isles.

—EDWARD LEAR
The Complete Nonsense

CHART 11-2. The IPA Diphthong [ɔɪ].

IPA Symbol	Sample	Type	Tongue	Lips or Mouth	Vocal Cords
ɔɪ	*oi*l	diph-thong	tip behind bottom front teeth, back arched toward hard palate for [ɔ], raising further toward hard palate for [ɪ]	lips rounded and a little protruding for [ɔ], closing and retracting for [ɪ]	vibrating

EXERCISE 48
[ɔɪ] *Diphthong Sound*

1. Using your mirror to watch the contrast in exaggerated lip positions, repeat ten times:

   r[ɔɪ]   w[i]   m[ɔɪ]   w[i]

2. Slowly pronounce the following words containing [ɔɪ]:

Initial	Medial	Final
oyster	disappoint	toy
oily	voice	employ
ointment	disjoint	enjoy
oyez	embroil	boy
oilcloth	rejoin	coy
oilbird	recoil	ploy

3. Read aloud the following pairs of words containing [ɔɪ]:

Roister Doister	rancid oil
soiled oilcloth	weak voice
boiling employer	recoilless rifle
toiling boys	misty void
foiled poisoner	soy sauce
moist cloister	ship ahoy
coy voice	growing boy
enjoyed toy	oyster stew

4. Match each word below with its correct phonetic counterpart. Sound each pair.

   1. toil _____ rɪdʒɔɪs
   2. soil _____ tɔɪ
   3. joist _____ cɔɪ
   4. voice _____ plɔɪ
   5. rejoice _____ bɔɪ

   6. toy _____ hɔɪ
   7. coy _____ vɔɪs
   8. ploy _____ dʒɔɪst
   9. boy _____ tɔɪl
   10. hoy _____ sɔɪl

5.   Read aloud the following sentences:

   1.   What kind of noise annoys an oyster?
   2.   The oily ointment spread over the moist oilcloth.
   3.   Roister Doister rolled up in a Rolls Royce.
   4.   Joy is unalloyed when it's not cloyed.
   5.   Townbee enjoyed toiling in the past.
   6.   A noisy noise annoys an oyster.
   7.   The employer disappointed the employee.
   8.   The coy boy lost his voice when he met the cowboy.
   9.   The noisome host hoisted his glass.
   10.   The hoi polloi refused to play according to Hoyle.

6.   Repeat as rapidly as possible with accuracy:

What kind of a noise annoys an oyster? A noisy noise
annoys an oyster.

> If somebody there chanced to be
> Who loved me in a manner true,
> My heart would point him out to me,
> And I would point him out to you.
> But here it says of those who point,
> Their manners must be out of joint—
> You *may* not point—
> You *must* not point—
> It's manners out of joint, to point!
>
> —W. S. GILBERT
> *Ruddigore*

> There was an old fellow from Roiling
> Whose temper was quick to come boiling;
> He'd leap and he'd hum as he banged on his drum,
> That boiling old Fellow from Roiling.
>
> —EDWARD LEAR
> *The Complete Nonsense*

CHART 11-3. The IPA Diphthong [aʊ].

IPA Symbol	Sample	Type	Tongue	Lips or Mouth	Vocal Cords
aʊ	cow	diph-thong	tip of tongue behind bottom front teeth, tongue flat in mouth for [a], arching upward for production of [ʊ]	open and relaxed for [a], closing and tightening for [ʊ]	vibrating

EXERCISE 49

[aʊ] *Dipthong Sound*

1. Using your mirror to watch the contrast in exaggerated lip positions, repeat ten times:

     r[aʊ]   w[i]   m[aʊ]   w[i]

2. Slowly pronounce the following words containing [aʊ]:

Initial	*Medial*	*Final*
oust	proud	how
ounce	shower	now
outlandish	blouse	cow
outwit	shout	allow
owl	brown	prow
outer	trowel	scow

3. Read aloud the following pairs of words containing [aʊ]:

     brown cow   squeaking mouse
     loud crowd   half ounce
     powwow   highbrow

> bounding hound   stray sow
> stone-ground flour   greasy towel
> dousing shower   proud prelate
> sounding vowels   down front
> flowery bower   out West

4. Match each word below with its correct phonetic counter-part. Sound each pair.

1. endow _____ taʊn
2. allow _____ əˈraʊnd
3. plow _____ ˈkɑmpaʊnd
4. sound _____ braʊn
5. abound _____ saʊ

6. town _____ əˈlaʊ
7. around _____ plaʊ
8. compound _____ saʊnd
9. brown _____ əˈbaʊnd
10. sow _____ ɪndaʊ

5. Read aloud the following sentences:

    1. Caesar was bound to refuse the crown.
    2. Down south the drought was about over.
    3. Be proud! Face the crowd! Be not bowed!
    4. When in doubt spout your thoughts aloud.
    5. The clown all in brown wore an angry frown.
    6. Around the mound they beat the ground yet never made a sound.
    7. The louse made its house on the mouse.
    8. The bouncer bounced the bounder into the bower.
    9. The bounty jumper was hounded across the boundary by the bounding hounds.
    10. A good, round sound is to be found downtown.

6. Repeat as rapidly as possible with accuracy:

> How now, brown cow?
>
> Up and down, and in and out,
> Here and there, and round about;
> Every chamber, every house,
> Every chink that holds a mouse.
>
> —W. S. GILBERT
> *The Yeomen of the Guard*

There was an Old Man with an owl,
Who continued to bother and howl;
He sate on a rail, and imbibed bitter ale,
Which refreshed that Old Man and his owl.

—EDWARD LEAR
The Complete Nonsense

12

Role-Playing for
Diction Evaluation

The role-playing exercises that follow are designed to provide
you with an opportunity to demonstrate control of diction in
situations where it will matter. You should study each situation
carefully; each exercise contains built-in goals you should try to
reach.

You may have to find a job, advise someone, explain a
lesson, sell a product, seek advice, or interview a job seeker.
Don't waste time planning what words to use; that is as useless
as planning speeches in the morning to carry you through the
day. Concentrate on your needs or goals, and the words, as in
real life, will take care of themselves.

During the semester you have been *listening* actively for
differences in sounds as well as for voice qualities. When you
are not actually in front of the class, use the following exercises
to test your listening ability. You, the listener, as well as the
speaker, should be working to improve your creative listening
faculty.

The ability to listen is to a great degree an index of speaking ability. During one class I asked a student what he thought
of a speech that had been delivered with many errors in diction.

He responded, "Poifect!" When each exercise is over, you should compare notes to see how well you listen. Remember, this is not a matinee theater, and you are not to conclude the exercise with a blank sheet of paper and the excuse that you were too absorbed to concentrate on diction.

Remember too, that your dictional evaluations are not offered to classmates as negative criticism; on the contrary, they represent constructive help that should aid the speakers to improve. The instructor may wish to collect your evaluation sheets to check out critical abilities. If so, each time an exercise is completed, write the speakers' names on a new sheet of paper. You will not be expected to hear everything—no one can do this—but if the entire class listens attentively, very little will escape notice. As a result, each speaker should receive a helpful and adequate dictional evaluation.

Your instructor may wish to assign the role-playing exercises a day or two in advance. Should this occur, never try to write out your part. You have no idea about what your partner will say or do, and you must react spontaneously and constructively. Use the time to prepare background material for your role-playing. Then if you are playing an authority, you will have facts to indicate your experience, and if you are playing an applicant, your needs can be clearly expressed.

EXERCISE 50
Role-Playing for Diction Evaluation

This exercise should be done by two persons at a time. The purpose is to check the diction when the control of diction is no longer the student's *primary* objective. When you perform this exercise before a class, borrow the instructor's desk for one participant, and place the other in a chair facing the class at the side of the desk.

1. Job Interview.
   Agree in advance on the identity of the company and the job opening, but do not agree on any more specifics.

Neither the applicant nor the interviewer should have any idea about what the other is going to say. Each, however, should prepare his part: the interviewer should know the personnel requirements; the applicant should know what questions to ask about the job and what strong points to bring forth to convince the interviewer—*if* he decides the job is desirable.

2. Student Counselling.

The counsellor should know the kind of school in which the counselling is to take place, but no more. The student should come in with a very specific problem which cannot be solved without the counsellor's help. He should not leave until the problem is satisfactorily solved.

3. Journalistic Interview.

Interviewer and interviewee should have a clear understanding of their roles and know the area of the interview, but nothing more. The situation can be adapted to occur between:

>   school newspaper reporter and dean concerning a school problem
>   school newspaper reporter and student officer
>   school newspaper reporter and professor
>   professional newspaper reporter and news source
>   television interviewer and politician
>   television interviewer and disaster witness or victim

4. Sales Pitch.

Arrange a situation in which the buyer wants to purchase something and the salesperson is adequately knowledgeable about the product. Or vary the situation so that the buyer has to be convinced. Or try letting the salesperson ring the door of an unprepared prospect and try to make a sale.

Other role-playing situations might include:

>   lawyer and trial witness
>   social worker and client
>   doctor and patient
>   investigating police officer and witness or suspect
>   parent and child

Please remember that you are not acting; consequently there is no demand for a complex character creation. Do not approach these exercises with a desire to entertain. They are tools for developing and practicing speech skills.

13

Achieving Variety on Your Musical Instrument

*I*magine you are about to buy a hi-fi set. You go into a store and, having been approached by a salesman, tell him of your errand. His eyes gleam with the expectation of a good commission.

You notice that he leads you toward the expensive corner of the store, passing by items with smaller sums on their price tags, and you stop and look at a low-priced model.

Salesman: That's not our better unit.

You: This is about the price I was thinking of spending.

Salesman: That's too bad, because this unit has a poor pitch range, and its tonal qualities are disappointing. It's really for the undiscerning.

You: What do you really mean by pitch range and tonal qualities?

Salesman: You get what you pay for. The pitch range is the distance between the low notes the model can sound and the high notes it can sound. The range on this cheaper model is not very good. Tone means the distinctive quality of the sound that gives resonance. The tone of a cheap set is light and tinny. It lacks fullness and *timbre*.

You: What do I get if I pay more?

Salesman: Our better sets will give you both a pitch range that offers the greatest differences between low and high notes, and a quality of tone that is rich, full, and resonant.

The salesman plays both sets for you, and the difference between the cheap and the expensive model is convincing. The cheap set lacks variety in pitch, has a Lilliputian range between low and high notes, and has no significant bass or treble selection difference. The better set has a full, resonant voice, with that quality of richness made up of blended deep, middle-range, and high notes. The sound spectrum is full, and listening to it is a satisfying auditory experience.

VOCAL QUALITY

Earlier we established that we speak with a musical instrument. Now it is time for you, keeping the criteria of the salesman concerning the hi-fi set in mind, to ask yourself what kind of an instrument you have been using. Is it weak and thin or rich and resonant? Perhaps you are confused by the question or do not know the quality of your own voice. Perhaps you are facing an unpleasant fact which you have always known but avoided thinking about: that your voice is weak, dull, or uninteresting. Have you realized that this may be why, at a party or a meeting when you wished very much to convey an idea, your idea was not given the proper attention?

Where does individual vocal quality come from, anyway? Why does one voice seem naturally good, while another seems naturally bad?

We have first to admit the validity of the genetic argument. You were born with a certain vocal potential. Your voice depends for its quality on the thickness of your vocal cords, the shape of your skull, the amount of flesh on your skull, the shape of your mouth and lips, the formation of your teeth, the thickness of your rib cage, the capacity of your lungs, and so on. With so many factors contributing to the production of your voice, no wonder it is as distinctive and unique as your finger-prints. Bell Telephone Laboratories can take vocal fingerprints, and they have reported that there is no such thing as two identical voices. But we all realize this. Have you ever tried to disguise your voice over the telephone, only to be told, "Come on, I know that's you!"

Let us be grateful that in this era of an expanding universe, giant corporations, super-sized governments, overpopulation, and statistics that predict our behavior, this is a piece of new evidence that we are all individuals, all unique. There will never be another you.

But what, you are asking, can you do about it if you were born with poor vocal equipment? How can you be made a more interesting and dynamic speaker? What can be done for the pitch and tone of your voice? Its strength and volume? The rate at which you speak?

Proper exercise work will improve pitch range and will teach you the correct pitch placement for your voice. In other words, you can discover whether your habitual or workaday pitch is on your optimum pitch level. I studied the Rocket Exercise for this purpose under the direction of a professional vocal coach who once worked with Laurence Olivier. You can, in time, improve the pitch range of your voice.

Can tone be altered? Only relatively, or partially, but this partial alteration can seem a miracle. Tone may be affected by many factors that cannot be changed, such as a sinus condition, thickness of the vocal cords, or chest resonance. The goal is to help you develop your best possible tone, and your best possible tone may be a vast improvement over your present tone.

You may seem to have weak vocal power, but there is no reason to be discouraged. We have all read the success stories of ballet dancers, tennis and baseball players, and ice skaters who took up their respective sports to strengthen damaged muscles, and who gradually through determination strengthened an already existent potential to the point where they became champions. The point is that at present you do not know your potential. One fact, though, is certain: everyone has a potentially full and interesting voice, no matter how small and weak it may be now.

Finally, this chapter can help you effectively to control the rate at which you speak. This is an important factor in achieving variety, and one that should never be overlooked. What is more pitiful than a speaker with a well-organized speech and a monotonous voice? How many times have you been mesmerized into an unthinking trance by a brilliant teacher who droned? How many capable political leaders have been lost to us because they had an uninteresting delivery on the platform? How many men, unworthy of our attention and our allegiance, have made it into the limelight on the strength of exciting oratorical technique alone?

PITCH AND TONE

Pitch is the frequency of a vibration. A rapidly vibrating object has a high frequency and can be described as high-pitched; a slowly vibrating object has a low frequency and can be described as low-pitched. The pitch range of your voice is the interval between the lowest note you can sound and the highest note you can sound. The pitch range of a piano, for instance, is found on its keyboard between the bottom and the top note. However a piano cannot change its pitch range, and you can.

The average, untrained person has a singing voice with a pitch range of two octaves or less, while a trained opera singer has a range of three or more octaves. The narrower your pitch range, the more monotonous and poor in tone is your voice. Horowitz, playing a concert, is only as good as the instrument provided him. Should the piano have a few octaves cut off its keyboard, the result would be crippling to the greatest artist. Some of us have vocal ranges that are crippling. I have heard students with vocal ranges that would enable them to execute nothing beyond "Hot Cross Buns."

Most individuals speak with voices that are too high-pitched. Their habitual pitch is above the *optimum pitch*, which is the point at which the voice is fullest and richest. This occurs because stress and pitch are related. A steel wire, tautened, will have a higher pitch than if it is slackened. In people, the tensions of living—the rush, the worry, the anxieties—tighten the entire body as well as the vocal cords and result sometimes in a highly pitched, taut voice.

We all enjoy listening to a well-modulated and low-pitched voice. Some actresses have cultivated what is called a bedroom voice. I would like to suggest that the compliment implies more than sex appeal. Try to think of how your voice sounds when you first wake up in the morning. Your body is totally relaxed; no tensions pull your vocal cords taut, and your voice is rich and full-bodied. But after dressing quickly and hurrying through breakfast, you pull open the front door and squeak a quick, "Goodbye!" In that short time your voice has responded to the tensions of modern living.

Relaxation in others attracts us. It seems to tell us that the relaxed person is stronger, more able to resist the tensions that beset us all, and we all admire strength.

Try the optimum pitch level test in Exercise 51. If you feel that your voice is pitched too high, return to the relaxation exercises in Chapter Two and work until you are able to recognize the condition of tightened vocal cords and learn to control it.

EXERCISE 51
Optimum Pitch Level Test

1. Block your ears with your fingers.
2. Reaching for a comfortable high note, slowly sing down the scale to a comfortable low note, then up again, finally down again. When you hear the note that sounds loudest to you, that note should be your optimum pitch.

If your habitual pitch level is above the note, as it is for most people, you have your work cut out for you. The Rocket Exercise, which follows, not only will help you to talk closer to

your optimum pitch level, it also will increase your pitch range
and resonance.

MEAN, MAIN, MINE, MOAN, MOON

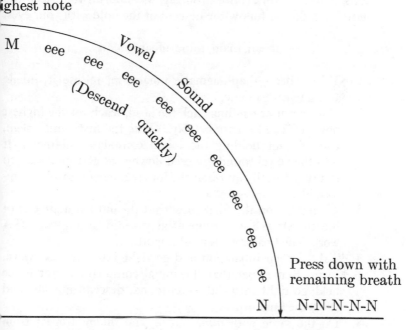

FIG. 13-1. Scale for Rocket Exercise

EXERCISE 52
Rocket Exercise
Tonal Improvement

Warning: This exercise is a vocal calisthenic and must be
practiced with caution. Hoarseness or vocal fatigue will follow
if you overdo at the beginning. If you feel signs of soreness,
stop. Practice for five minutes at first, and gradually increase to
ten minutes.

Practicing this exercise will produce noise, so you should

find an appropriate place to work and disregard kibitzers. You will have to work diligently, and usually it will take two months before noticeable results from this exercise appear; but the results, if you do work conscientiously, will impress you. Keep the head level; do not follow the descent of the note with your eyes.

mean, main, mine, moan, moon

1. Take a deep, diaphragmatic inhalation, release it, inhale again, release, inhale.
2. Now, without bending back the head, reach for the highest note you can hit *comfortably*.* Take the first word, *mean*, and without holding the initial consonant, sliding right into the vowel sound, proceed downward at a moderate to fast speed until you reach the lowest note you can hit comfortably.
3. Then press on the final consonant [n] until you are out of breath. Stress the consonant as you did during your IPA work. The final press is most important.
4. Take a deep inhalation and go right into the next word, *main*. Remember that the initial consonant is not to be held; go right into the vowel sound, descend quickly, and stress the final [n].
5. Do the same with *mine*, *moan*, and *moon*. Repeat from the beginning until you have exercised for the desired amount of time.

This exercise is designed literally to stretch the vocal cords.

EXERCISE 53

Tonal Improvement

This is another exercise for tonal improvement. In order to get fuller vibrations from your entire instrument, it is necessary

---

* If this high note falls within your falsetto range, you will find in gliding downward that you must ride over a vocal ridge, the nodule on which yodelers work when they yodel. Do not let this phenomenon disturb you.

to make your bass, middle, and upper registers vibrate. This exercise is to increase vocal flexibility.

1. Yawn as in the Rag Doll Exercise (Exercise 4) and while yawning, think of a hot liquid—tea or soup—pouring down your throat. This relaxes the vocal cords.
2. Take a deep breath and try to sound the note you have established as your optimum pitch, saying "ah" and holding it for the duration of the breath. Repeat ten times, taking a full inhalation each time.
3. Now yawn and say *hello* ten times, on your optimum pitch level.
4. Yawn and speak any sentence you choose to invent or read, remembering the sensation of hot liquid in the throat or the sensation of yawning. If you possibly can, tape your voice while doing the above and contrast it to a tape of your habitual voice, when you are not making a conscious effort to speak at your optimum pitch. You will find that the difference in voices is significant.

EXERCISE 54
Tonal Variety

1. Read the excerpt below from *Alice in Wonderland*. Then read it aloud, trying to give each character a distinctive voice. Reread it aloud several times, experimenting with your voice; explore your instrument and find out what it can do. This is an exercise, and not a performance. Remember, each character has a voice of his own.

A Mad Tea-Party

There was a table set out under a tree in front of the house, and the March Hare and the Hatter were having tea at it: a Dormouse was sitting between them, fast asleep, and the other two were using it as a cushion, resting their elbows on it, and talking over its head. "Very uncomfortable for the

Dormouse," thought Alice; "only as it's asleep, I suppose it doesn't mind."

The table was a large one, but the three were all crowded together at one corner of it. "No room! No room!" they cried out when they saw Alice coming. "There's *plenty* of room!" said Alice indignantly, and she sat down in a large arm-chair at one end of the table.

"Have some wine," the March Hare said in an encouraging tone.

Alice looked all round the table, but there was nothing on it but tea. "I don't see any wine," she remarked.

"There isn't any," said the March Hare.

"Then it wasn't very civil of you to offer it," said Alice angrily.

"It wasn't very civil of you to sit down without being invited," said the March Hare.

"I didn't know it was *your* table," said Alice: "it's laid for a great many more than three."

"Your hair wants cutting," said the Hatter. He had been looking at Alice for some time with great curiosity, and this was his first speech.

"You should learn not to make personal remarks," Alice said with some severity: "It's very rude."

The Hatter opened his eyes very wide on hearing this; but all he *said* was, "Why is a raven like a writing desk?"

"Come, we shall have some fun now!" thought Alice. "I'm glad they've begun asking riddles—I believe I can guess that," she added aloud.

"Do you mean that you think you can find out the answer to it?" said the March Hare.

"Exactly so," said Alice.

"Then you should say what you mean," the March Hare went on.

"I do," Alice hastily replied; "at least—at least I mean what I say—that's the same thing, you know."

"Not the same thing a bit!" said the Hatter. "Why, you might just as well say that 'I see what I eat' is the same thing as 'I eat what I see'!"

"You might just as well say," added the March Hare,

"that 'I like what I get' is the same thing as 'I get what I like'!"

"You might just as well say," added the Dormouse, which seemed to be talking in its sleep, "that 'I breathe when I sleep' is the same thing as 'I sleep when I breathe'!"

"It *is* the same thing with you," said the Hatter, and here the conversation dropped, and the party sat silent for a minute, while Alice thought over all she could remember about ravens and writing-desks, which wasn't much.

The Hatter was the first to break the silence. "What day of the month is it?" he said, turning to Alice: he had taken his watch out of his pocket, and was looking at it uneasily, shaking it every now and then, and holding it to his ear.

Alice considered a little, and then said, "The fourth."

"Two days wrong!" sighed the Hatter. "I told you butter wouldn't suit the works!" he added, looking angrily at the March Hare.

"It was the *best* butter," the March Hare meekly replied.

"Yes, but some crumbs must have got in as well," the Hatter grumbled: "you shouldn't have put it in with the bread-knife."

The March Hare took the watch and looked at it gloomily: then he dipped it into his cup of tea, and looked at it again: but he could think of nothing better to say than his first remark, "It was the *best* butter, you know."

Alice had been looking over his shoulder with some curiosity. "What a funny watch!" she remarked. "It tells the day of the month, and doesn't tell what o'clock it is!"

"Why should it?" muttered the Hatter. "Does *your* watch tell you what year it is?"

"Of course not," Alice replied very readily: "but that's because it stays the same year for such a long time together."

"Which is just the case with *mine*," said the Hatter.

Alice felt dreadfully puzzled. The Hatter's remark seemed to her to have no sort of meaning in it, and yet it was certainly English. "I don't quite understand you," she said, as politely as she could.

"The Dormouse is asleep again," said the Hatter, and he poured a little hot tea upon its nose.

The Dormouse shook its head impatiently, and said,

without opening its eyes, "Of course, of course: just what I was going to remark myself."

—LEWIS CARROLL
Alice's Adventures in Wonderland

VOLUME

Volume is best understood in terms of force or energy. But to learn to control volume it is not enough to think in terms of maximum loudness; loudness is a meaningless concept except by contrast with softness. The volume control knob on a hi-fi set can be used to play softly, loudly, or anywhere in between. Being able to produce a lowering of energy and forcefulness in your voice is vital to the achievement of variety.

Vocal energy is generated in the diaphragm. It is therefore important to have a strong diaphragm.

EXERCISE 55
The Dolphin

Basic Yoga Exercise for Strengthening of Diaphragm

1. Kneel on the floor on a carpet, mat, or blanket. Knit your fingers behind your head and lean forward until your head is on the floor. With your hands still laced behind your head, bring your elbows down to the floor.
2. Extend your legs behind you and go up on your toes. Your body should be forming an inverted *v*.
3. Gravity is pulling on your abdominal cavity and your diaphragm. With mouth open, jerk your diaphragm quickly up toward your spinal cord. Release it quickly and pull it

back up quickly. Imitate a dog's panting on a hot day, contracting and releasing the diaphragm with each pant. Start with twenty-five contractions and increase in a few days to thirty-five, then to fifty. Try eventually to reach one hundred contractions.

This exercise is relaxing and it greatly strengthens the diaphragm. If you have flabby stomach muscles, it will do wonders for them, too.

EXERCISE 56

Breath Control

Breath control really means diaphragmatic control. If you have difficulty with this exercise, return to Exercise 55 for strengthening the diaphragm. A properly strengthened diaphragm will prevent the kind of speech problem that arises when the speaker's sentences fade away into inaudibility.

1. Read the following without rushing as the sentences grow in length. Keep the same moderate and regular pace throughout.

The House That Jack Built

(*Inhale*). This is the house that Jack built. (*Exhale.*)
(*Inhale*). This is the malt that lay in the house that Jack built. (*Exhale.*)
(*Inhale*). This is the rat that ate the malt that lay in the house that Jack built. (*Exhale.*)
(*Inhale*). This is the cat that killed the rat that ate the malt that lay in the house that Jack built. (*Exhale.*)
(*Inhale*). This is the dog that worried the cat that killed the rat that ate the malt that lay in the house that Jack built. (*Exhale.*)
(*Inhale*). This is the cow with the crumpled horn that tossed the dog that worried the cat that killed the

rat that ate the malt that lay in the house that Jack built. (*Exhale.*)

(*Inhale*). This is the milkmaid all forlorn who milked the cow with the crumpled horn that tossed the dog that worried the cat that killed the rat that ate the malt that lay in the house that Jack built. (*Exhale.*)

(*Inhale*). This is the man all tattered and torn who kissed the milkmaid all forlorn who milked the cow with the crumpled horn that tossed the dog that worried the cat that killed the rat that ate the malt that lay in the house that Jack built. (*Exhale.*)

(*Inhale*). This is the priest all shaven and shorn who married the man all tattered and torn who kissed the milkmaid all forlorn who milked the cow with the crumpled horn that tossed the dog that worried the cat that killed the rat that ate the malt that lay in the house that Jack built. (*Exhale.*)

(*Inhale*). This is the cock that crowed in the morn that waked the priest all shaven and shorn who married the man all tattered and torn who kissed the milkmaid all forlorn who milked the cow with the crumpled horn that tossed the dog that worried the cat that killed the rat that ate the malt that lay in the house that Jack built! (*Any breath left to exhale?*)

EXERCISE 57

Vocal Energy

The object of this exercise is a full release of vocal energy. It is necessary, however, to warm up to this full release, which is the reason for the first two steps of the exercise.

1. Do the Rag Doll Exercise (Exercise 4).
2. Do a few Rocket Exercise slides (Exercise 52).
3. Jerking your diaphgram in rapidly, as in Exercise 55, vocalize one syllable ("Ho!") on each contraction. Take a full

inhalation before each "Ho!" and vocalize as contracting diaphragm pushes air back out.

(quickly and softly)	Ho! Ho! Ho! Ho!
(somewhat louder)	Ho! Ho! Ho! Ho!
(again louder)	Ho! Ho! Ho! Ho!
(very loud, fullest energy)	Ho! Ho! Ho! Ho!

4. Repeat Step 3 in reverse, proceeding from very loud to soft.

EXERCISE 58
Volume Control

1. Take a full inhalation and, at your optimum pitch level, say *one* very quietly, holding the [n] until all the air is exhaled from your lungs.
2. Take another deep breath and say *two* a little louder but at the same pitch, holding the final vowel sound until all the air is expelled.
3. Taking a full inhalation before each number, increase the volume for *three, four,* and *five,* remembering to keep the pitch constant. If the pitch rises, stop and begin on your optimum pitch level.
4. Reverse the procedure, going from a loud *five* to an almost whispered *one.*

EXERCISE 59
Volume and Projection

Environment is a most important element in any speaking situation. Conversation in a rapidly moving subway car is held on a different level of volume from a conversation over a small, candlelit table. Most of my readers are probably confined to one classroom during the entire speech course. I suggest that for this exercise the environment be changed. Move to a larger room, an auditorium, a gym, or out-of-doors to the football field or baseball diamond. Try to find more challenging surroundings, as Demosthenes did when he went to the surf.

1. Take a deep breath before starting, and sustain the following phrases for as long as you can make your breath last. Do not rush the sounds. Think of speed as your enemy and stretch, sustain, have a taffy pull with the sounds, holding them for ten, fifteen, or more seconds apiece. Have fun; use full energy. If you are part of a class, ask the class to set up a competitive rumble and call out:

   L-a-d-i-e-s a-n-d g-e-n-t-l-e-m-e-n, m-a-y I h-a-v-e y-o-u-r a-t-t-e-n-t-i-o-n, p-l-e-a-s-e?
   H-e-l-p! H-e-l-p!
   F-r-i-e-n-d-s, R-o-m-a-n-s, c-o-u-n-t-r-y-m-e-n, l-e-n-d m-e y-o-u-r e-a-r-s!

2. The next reading provides an excellent opportunity to practice variety of volume. You will need an ordinary reading tone for the narration, a variety of crescendoes for the queen's outbursts, and a quiet tone for the king's timid remarks, as well as the appropriate volume range for Alice's contributions. Practice adjusting volume and remember that volume does not always mean loudness—it simply means *amount* of loudness, which can in fact be very little. The volume knob on a stereo lowers as well as raises. Read the excerpt carefully once or twice; then cut loose.

   Alice was rather doubtful whether she ought not to lie down on her face like the three gardeners, but she could not remember ever having heard of such a rule at processions; "And besides, what would be the use of a procession," thought she, "if people had all to lie down on their faces, so that they couldn't see it?" So she stood where she was, and waited.
   When the procession came opposite to Alice, they all stopped and looked at her, and the Queen said, severely, "Who

is this?" She said it to the Knave of Hearts, who only bowed and smiled in reply.

"Idiot!" said the Queen, tossing her head impatiently; and, turning to Alice, she went on: "What's your name, child?"

"My name is Alice, so please your Majesty," said Alice very politely; but she added, to herself, "Why, they're only a pack of cards, after all. I needn't be afraid of them!"

"And who are *these?*" said the Queen, pointing to the three gardeners who were lying round the rose-tree; for, you see, as they were lying on their faces, and the pattern on their backs was the same as the rest of the pack, she could not tell whether they were gardeners, or soldiers, or courtiers, or three of her own children.

"How should *I* know?" said Alice, surprised at her own courage. "It's no business of *mine.*"

The Queen turned crimson with fury, and, after glaring at her for a moment like a wild beast, began screaming, "Off with her head! Off with—"

"Nonsense!" said Alice, very loudly and decidedly, and the Queen was silent.

The King laid his hand upon her arm, and timidly said, "Consider, my dear: she is only a child!"

The Queen turned angrily away from him, and said to the Knave, "Turn them over!"

The Knave did so, very carefully, with one foot.

"Get up!" said the Queen in a shrill, loud voice, and the three gardeners instantly jumped up, and began bowing to the King, the Queen, the royal children, and everybody else.

"Leave off that!" screamed the Queen. "You make me giddy." And then, turning to the rose-tree, she went on, "What *have* you been doing here?"

"May it please your Majesty," said Two, in a very humble tone, going down on one knee as he spoke, "we were trying—"

"*I* see!" said the Queen, who had meanwhile been examining the roses. "Off with their heads!" and the procession moved on, three of the soldiers remaining behind to execute the unfortunate gardeners, who ran to Alice for protection.

"You shan't be beheaded!" said Alice, and she put them

into a large flower-pot that stood near. The three soldiers wandered about for a minute or two, looking for them, and then quietly marched off after the others.

"Are their heads off?" shouted the Queen.

"Their heads are gone, if it please your Majesty!" the soldiers shouted in reply.

"That's right!" shouted the Queen. "Can you play croquet?"

The soldiers were silent, and looked at Alice, as the question was evidently meant for her.

"Yes!" shouted Alice.

"Come on, then!" roared the Queen, and Alice joined the procession, wondering very much what would happen next.

—LEWIS CARROLL
Alice's Adventures in Wonderland

RATE

It is time to return to the girl whom we left on the first page of Chapter One. She had been told to slow down, but had been offered not a technique but an injunction: "Go slower!" How should she have slowed down?

If you had never driven a car or seen one driven and were put behind the wheel of a moving vehicle and told to go slower, all the desire in the world to comply could not help you until you were shown the brake. Brakes operate on the scientific principle that friction impedes movement; and as all physical bodies on earth are subject to the laws of physics, it is predictably possible to slow speech scientifically by the application of friction. When we realize that by the nature of their origin the consonant sounds of our speech are our friction sounds, we can see that by "stepping on" the consonants, or pronouncing them more carefully and meticulously, we can create enough friction to slow down the fastest speech.

The benefits from the following exercise are threefold. Properly practiced, this exercise *will* slow you down. It will help to rid you of mumbled or sloppy speech. It will enable you to hear yourself, without benefit of tape recorder. When you are chanting you can *hear* yourself in a new way because you are speaking in slow motion, and you can correct the distorted vowel or mangled consonant. The exercise virtually provides you with a built-in tape recorder. It also allows you time to *think out* the proper placement of lips and tongue in order to break poor speech habits.

It may have one other effect: it may give you a hearty appreciation of George Bernard Shaw's desire to make the spelling of English phonetic. When you are proceeding at an abnormally slow rate, you may find yourself pronouncing *is* as *iss*. You may wonder why it should not be spelled *iz*.

EXERCISE 60
Chanting

While reading the passage from Plato which follows, observe these instructions:

1. Hold or stress every consonant that can be held for four seconds. (Remember that plosives, by their very explosive nature, cannot be held, so pronounce but do not hold [p], [b], [t], [d], [k], [g], and the plosive-fricative combinations [dʒ] and [tʃ].) You have practiced the holding of consonants in the IPA exercises; the easiest holding method is to tap four fingers successively and rhythmically on a table, or to lift up your hand and fold the fingers down successively. Remember also to sound the consonants purely, without anticipating the vowels that follow. Say "mmmmmmmm" rather than "meeeeee" or "maaaaaa," and "rrrrrrr" rather than "reeeeeee."

2. Hold or stress all vowel sounds that are normally sounded for two seconds, or half as long as consonants. Tap or fold fingers, maintaining a regular rhythm.

3. All words must be chanted exactly as pronounced. This is important, and sometimes difficult. The consonants have been underlined with four lines and the vowels with two. Silent, unpronounced letters have been left unmarked, and plosive and plosive-fricative sounds which cannot be held have been marked with an x.

4. Before beginning the passage, chant sample words:

bath   is   of

bathe   us   off

5. Now chant the passage from Plato.

The body is a source of endless trouble to us by reason of the mere requirement of food; and is liable also to diseases which overtake and impede us in the search after true being; it fills us full of loves, and lusts, and fears, and fancies of all kinds, and endless foolery, and in fact, as men say, takes away from us the power of thinking at all. Whence comes wars, and fighting, and factions? Where but from the body and the lusts of the body? Wars are occasioned by the love of money, and money has to be acquired for the sake and in the service of the body; and by reason of all these impediments we have no time to give to philosophy; and last and worst of all, even if we are at leisure and betake ourselves to some speculation, the body is always breaking in upon us, causing turmoil and confusion in our enquiries, and so amazing us that we are prevented from seeing the truth.

—Plato
Phaedo

EXERCISE 61
Variety in Rate

1. Read this selection at a varied rate, trying to make it interesting. When you get to the last section beginning, "You're a regular wreck," accelerate as much as you can.

> When you're lying awake with a dismal headache, and repose is taboo'd by anxiety,
> I conceive you may use any language you choose to indulge in, without impropriety;
> For your brain is on fire—the bedclothes conspire of usual slumber to plunder you:
> First your counterpane goes, and uncovers your toes, and your sheet slips demurely from under you;
> Then the blanketing tickles—you feel like mixed pickles —so terribly sharp is the pricking,
> And you're hot, and you're cross, and you tumble and toss till there's nothing 'twixt you and the ticking.
> Then the bedclothes all creep to the ground in a heap, and you pick 'em all up in a tangle;
> Next your pillow resigns and politely declines to remain at its usual angle!
> Well, you get some repose in the form of a doze, with hot eye-balls and head ever aching,
> But your slumbering teems with such horrible dreams that you'd very much better be waking;
> For you dream you are crossing the Channel, and tossing about in a steamer from Harwich—
> Which is something between a large bathing machine and a very small second-class carriage—
> And you're giving a treat (penny ice and cold meat) to a party of friends and relations—
> They're a ravenous horde—and they all came on board at Sloane Square and South Kensington Stations.
> And bound on that journey you find your attorney (who started that morning from Devon);

He's a bit undersized, and you don't feel surprised when
     he tells you he's only eleven.

Well, you're driving like mad with this singular lad (by
     the by, the ship's now a four-wheeler),

And you're playing round games, and he calls you bad
     names when you tell him that "ties pay the dealer";

But this you can't stand, so you throw up your hand, and
     you find you're as cold as an icicle,

In your shirt and your socks (the black silk with gold
     clocks), crossing Salisbury Plain on a bicycle:

And he and the crew are on bicycles too—which they've
     somehow or other invested in—

And he's telling the tars all the particulars of a company
     he's interested in—

It's a scheme of devices, to get at low prices all goods
     from cough mixtures to cables

(Which tickled the sailors), by treating retailers as
     though they were all vegetables—

You get a good spadesman to plant a small tradesman
     (first take off his boots with a boot-tree),

And his legs will take root, and his fingers will shoot,
     and they'll blossom and bud like a fruit-tree—

From the greengrocer tree you get grapes and green pea,
     cauliflower, pineapple, and cranberries,

While the pastrycook plant cherry brandy will grant,
     apple puffs, and three-corners, and Banburys—

The shares are a penny, and ever so many are taken by
     Rothschild and Baring,

And just as a few are allotted to you, you awake with a
     shudder despairing—

You're a regular wreck, with a crick in your neck, and
     no wonder you snore, for your head's on the floor,
     and you've needles and pins from your soles to your
     shins, and your flesh is a-creep, for your left leg's
     asleep, and you've cramp in your toes, and a fly on
     your nose, and some fluff in your lung, and a fever-
     ish tongue, and a thirst that's intense, and a general
     sense that you haven't been sleeping in clover;

But the darkness has passed, and it's daylight at last, and
the night has been long—ditto ditto my song—and
thank goodness they're both of them over!

—W. S. GILBERT
Iolanthe

PAUSES

Pauses are to speech what loudness is to softness; the two
opposites give each other more significance. A musical composition, if it is of any length, employs varied tempos; it also makes
considerable use of the pause or "rest."

The beginning speaker is in awe of the pause, thinking, "If I
stop for a moment, I'll lose my audience!" Actually the opposite
is true. If he does *not* stop, he will lose his audience. A pause at
the right time gives the audience the important moment it needs
to think, and to get involved with what the speaker is saying. A
pause also gives the speaker the opportunity to change volume,
rate, or pitch.

Pause, for instance, after asking a question. Give your audience a chance to answer mentally. That moment of involvement
on the part of the audience means success to you. But during
your pause keep eye contact with the audience; keep projecting
your own attitude. Do not make the mistake of asking the
question and then turning away to take a drink or consult your
notes. Remember that there is both a *controlled* pause—a pause
of which *you* are in control—and an *empty* pause—a pause that is
void of your personal impact. Produce a controlled pause, not an
empty one.

The controlled pause can be an enormously effective
moment during which you charge the atmosphere with your
personality and reaffirm whatever it is you are supporting. I have
had many students object to me that in their speeches they are
supporting *no* ideas, have *no* point of view. But—unless you are

presenting a simple committee report—whether you are debating, running for office, or presenting an after-dinner speaker, you *must* have a point of view, even if it is only, "I am so proud to be presenting the best possible speaker in the whole world to you."

Remember also to let pauses occur in terms of ideas; follow a major idea with a pause before beginning on new material. Then convey the idea that it is new material with a shift in tempo and volume. The thought pattern of your material may have little relationship to its commas and periods, so be alert and independent.

EXERCISE 62
Pauses

1. In the following passage, pause after each question to give your listener a chance to make a mental response. Experiment with the duration of the pauses. Will they all be of the same duration? Remember that interpretation can only be a matter of intelligence and taste, that there can be no one single answer that is "correct," and let the logic and inner truth work from the text. The only test of your interpretation is its effectiveness.

> Are you the new person drawn toward me, and asking
> something significant from me?
> To begin with, take warning—I am probably far
> different from what you suppose;
> Do you suppose you will find in me your ideal?
> Do you think it so easy to have me become your lover?
> Do you think the friendship of me would be
> unalloyed satisfaction?
> Do you suppose I am trusty and faithful?
> Do you see no further than this facade—this smooth
> and tolerant manner of me?
> Do you suppose yourself advancing on real ground
> toward a real heroic man?

Have you no thought, O dreamer, that it may be all
    maya, illusion? O the next step may precipitate you!
O let some past deceived one hiss in your ears, how
    many have prest on the same
    as you are pressing now,
How many have fondly supposed what you are
    supposing now—only to be disappointed.

—WALT WHITMAN
Leaves of Grass

2. Read the passage below trying to use effectual pauses. It will seem unnatural, perhaps, pausing after every "Will you?" and "Won't you?" but try it anyway, as an exercise. See how interesting you can make this short passage sound. Will you? (Pause.) Won't you? (Pause).

"Will you walk a little faster?" said a whiting to a snail,
"There's a porpoise close behind us, and he's treading on
    my tail.
See how eagerly the lobsters and the turtles all advance!
They are waiting on the shingle—will you come and join
    the dance?
    Will you, won't you, will you, won't you, will you join
    the dance?
    Will you, won't you, will you, won't you, won't you
    join the dance?
"You can really have no notion how delightful it will be
When they take us up and throw us, with the lobsters,
    out to sea!"
But the snail replied, "Too far, too far!" and gave a look
    askance—
Said he thanked the whiting kindly, but he would not
    join the dance.
    Would not, could not, would not, could not, would
    not join the dance.
    Would not, could not, would not, could not, could
    not join the dance.
"What matters it how far we go?" his scaly friend re-
    plied.

"There is another shore, you know, upon the other side.
The farther off from England the nearer is to France—
Then turn not pale, beloved snail, but come and join
the dance.
   Will you, won't you, will you, won't you, will you join
   the dance?
   Will you, won't you, will you, won't you, won't you
   join the dance?"

—LEWIS CARROLL
Alice's Adventures in Wonderland

14

Content and Interpretation

It was demonstrated in the last chapter that you can control four elements in an attempt to achieve variety in speech: pitch, volume, rate, and pauses. Now how are you going to use this control when you make a speech? You do not vary these elements at random, simply for the sake of variation. What *dictates* a change in rate, pitch, volume?

If your voice is an instrument, your text is the composition you are to play. A composer uses tempo and volume changes, and changes of key as well, to project moods, emotions, or feelings. We are concerned with the same elements, and we must also project varied feelings in our speeches if we are to avoid monotony.

This brings us to the question of interpretation. Anyone intelligent enough to be in college is capable of getting at the meaning in a piece of writing. But man comprehends in two distinct ways, emotionally and intellectually. Getting at the meaning is not enough; the speaker must express and evoke appropriate emotional responses.

Earlier I referred to great speakers of history and the command they had over their speaking instruments. All of these men had, above all, the ability to discover an appropriate emotional attitude when they spoke, and then to project that attitude toward the audience.

Will anyone who witnessed the event, or even heard about it, forget the moment when Nikita Khrushchev took off his shoe in the United Nations assembly, banged it on the table, and shouted, "We will bury you and your children!" He projected both his anger and his threat. Yet the incident may have been carefully prepared and stage-managed, just as Adolf Hitler's appearances—in the middle of an enormous stadium, with Hitler spotlighted on the top of a marble shaft—were carefully arranged for maximum emotional effect. Fidel Castro has the same ability to arouse the emotions; so had Benito Mussolini. What was the real, emotional effect of Khrushchev's behavior? Wasn't our reaction what he wanted: fear, because "a man who will do a thing like that, something that just isn't done, might do anything!"

Compare, in Shakespeare, the success of Mark Anthony to the failure of Gaius Coriolanus. Mark Anthony was not too proud to manipulate a crowd by putting on public display the bloody wounds of his friend, while the pride and integrity of Coriolanus, a worthier man, prevented him from seeking popularity by displaying his own wounds won in battle. Coriolanus demanded instead a purely intellectual appreciation—a cold commodity. Or read Plato's account of the trial of Socrates to see how logic can be defeated by emotion. It is important to know how to project emotions if you are to speak successfully.

Often at this point a student will protest to me, "What are you trying to do, make actors of us? I can't act!"

PUBLIC SPEAKING VERSUS ACTING

Public speaking, debating, or simple reading to others, all have one factor in common with acting: one is speaking before a group of people. But here the similarity ends. Acting is a complex art that involves the entire mind and body in characterization, makeup, a relationship to the director, scenery, props, the other actors, stage business, and many other factors. But we are concerned here only with the voice, and to a minor extent with the body, as an instrument. In this one way, then, you must be like an actor: you must use your instrument to convey your emotions.

Imagine that a woman's house is on fire. It is late at night; her sleeping children are in danger; she runs to a window to call for help; and her voice comes to us in a deep, low, breathy tone: "Help."

Ridiculous! We expect her emotions to make her body rigid with fear, her vocal cords taut with tension; and we expect her voice to emerge in a high-pitched scream: "He-e-e-l-p!" The voice must be appropriate to the material.

Let us say that you have chosen your material. Never attempt an immediate oral reading of it. First read it carefully for its central idea or theme. I have seen many students plunge into an oral interpretation or even a delivery of a personally written speech without proper preparation. Examine the material. Paraphrase it in your own words. Take your time, being suspicious of the first easy answer to your questions. Try to get at the author's exact meaning rather than to create one of your own.

First ask yourself, "What is the overall message and its accompanying mood?" Is it, for instance, happy, sad, peaceful, angry, loving, full of hate, humble, proud, panegyric, satiric, revolutionary, reactionary, sensual, cold, respectful, disrespectful, religious, irreverent, honest, dishonest, secretive, open, flirtatious, prim, calm, unruly?

Next, you must relate the controllable elements of speech to the emotions you want to project. For instance, look at the suggestions in the table below. They do not represent fixed rules in any way; they are nothing but very broad suggestions. You might make a far more effective communication of happiness by *slowing* your rate and *lowering* your volume, in a particular text, than by increasing rate and volume.

Emotion	Rate	Volume	Pitch
happiness	faster	louder	higher
sadness	slower	softer	lower
anguish	faster	louder	higher
secretiveness	slower	softer	lower
sensuality	slower	softer	lower
anger	faster	louder	higher

While there is no one *right* way to interpret emotion, it is important to think of the theme or mood in terms transferable into action by your instrument.

CREATIVE INTERPRETATION

Once you have captured the main idea, or theme, take the next creative step by marking the material as a musician might mark a score. You might use a code such as *F* and *S* for faster and slower; one underscore for lower, two for louder, and three for loudest; an arrow pointing up for heightened pitch and one pointing down for lowered pitch; one vertical line for a short pause, two for a moderate pause, and three for a considerable pause.

As an example let us take a familiar, short poem, Wordsworth's "The World Is Too Much with Us."

I interpret the poem to myself, saying that the poet has taken a philosophical point of view that people are too materialistic. He makes a judgment for the first eight and one-half lines of the poem, and a passionate dissension in the last five and one-half lines. He translates his intellectual judgment into many particular and concrete images which evoke emotions. He implies a strong criticism of contemporary man's religion, which seems to have failed him, and says he would prefer to be a pagan who knew enough to worship nature, rather than money. He is throughout nothing if not emphatic.

Having made these comments to myself, I mark the poem:

The world is too much with us; | late and soon, |
　　　S　　　　　　　　　　　　F

Getting and spending, | we lay waste our powers: ||
　　F　　　　　　　　　F
　　louder　　　　　　　　loudest

Little we see in Nature that is ours; ||

We have given our hearts away, || a sordid boon! |||
　　　　　　　　　　　　　　　S

This sea that bares her bosom to the moon; |
　　S

The winds that will be howling at all hours, |
　　F

And are up-gathered now like sleeping flowers; |
　　S

For this! | for everything! | we are out of tune;
　　　　build in volume

It moves us not. || — Great God! | I'd rather be
　louder　　　　　full volume

A Pagan suckled in a creed outworn; |
　　S

So might I, | standing on this pleasant lea,

Have glimpses that would make me less forlorn; ||

Have sight of Proteus rising from the sea; |

Or hear old Triton blow his wreathèd horn.
　　　S

Try following this sort of marking system; but just as important, try making your own.

I conclude this section with some selections for you to experiment on. They have been gathered purely for your convenience, and only as a start. Remember, once you have done your mental paraphrasing and have dug out the subject or meaning, to mark the material with interpretative signs that mean something to you.

Next should come the very important step of practicing the interpretation on your instrument over and over to make sure you really *do* increase the volume, decrease the rate, pause effectively, change pitch smoothly, and so on.

Don't fall into the Walter Mitty trap of delivering a well-prepared oral interpretation *silently* to yourself, imagining a magnificent, soaring voice here, deep tones there, and applause at the conclusion while the impressed instructor wrings your hand. Suppose you were to enter a room to find a music student seated at a fine piano, bent over a well-annotated score that shows a lot of work has gone into understanding and interpreting the music. The student, arms folded, is swaying back and forth rhythmically to the strains of the imagined music. "What are you doing?" "Practicing this music." "When will you play it?" "Tomorrow, at the concert."

Incredible as this may sound, too many speech students prepare their work in just this way, and are upset when their sincere efforts are not applauded. Remember, you are preparing to speak with a musical instrument. Use your instrument to prepare.

READING SELECTIONS

Henry David Thoreau, extract from Journals

May 1, 1857

It is foolish for a man to accumulate material wealth chiefly, houses and land. Our stock in life, our real estate, is that amount of thought which we have had, which we have thought out. The ground we have thus created is forever pasturage for our thoughts. I fall back on to visions which I have had. What else adds to my possessions and makes me rich in all lands? If you have ever done any work with these finest tools, the imagination and fancy and reason, it is a new creation, independent of the world and a possession forever. You have laid up something against a rainy day. You have to that extent cleared the wilderness.

Walt Whitman, from Leaves of Grass

Music always round me, unceasing, unbeginning—yet
long untaught I did not hear,
But now the chorus I hear, and am elated.
A tenor, strong, ascending, with power and health, with
glad notes of day-break I hear,
A soprano, at intervals, sailing buoyantly over the tops of
immense waves,
A transparent bass, shuddering lusciously under and
through the universe,
A triumphant tutti—the funeral wailings, with sweet
flutes and violins—All these I fill myself with;
I hear not the volumes of sound merely—I am moved by
the exquisite meanings.

Charles Dickens, extract from Oliver Twist

The room in which the boys were fed, was a large stone hall, with a copper at one end: out of which the master, dressed in an apron for the purpose, and assisted by one or two women, ladled the gruel at meal-times. Of this festive composition each boy had one porringer, and no more—except on occasions of great public rejoicing, when he had two ounces and a quarter of bread besides. The bowls never wanted washing. The boys polished them with their spoons till they shone again; and when they had performed this operation (which never took very long, the spoons being nearly as large as the bowls), they would sit staring at the copper, with such eager eyes, as if they could have devoured the very bricks of which it was composed; employing themselves, meanwhile, in sucking their fingers most assiduously, with the view of catching up any stray splashes of gruel that might have been cast thereon. Boys have generally excellent appetites. Oliver Twist and his companions suffered the tortures of slow starvation for three months; at last they got so voracious and wild with hunger, that one boy, who was tall for his age, and hadn't been used to that sort of thing (for his father had kept a small cook-shop), hinted darkly to his companions, that unless he had another basin of gruel *per diem*, he was afraid he might some night happen to eat the boy who slept next him, who happened to be a weakly youth of tender age. He had a wild, hungry eye; and they implicitly believed him. A council was held; lots were cast who should walk up to the master after supper that evening, and ask for more, and it fell to Oliver Twist.

The evening arrived; the boys took their places. The master, in his cook's uniform, stationed himself at the copper; his pauper assistants ranged themselves behind him; the gruel was served out; and a long grace was said over the short commons. The gruel disappeared; the boys whispered each other, and winked at Oliver; while his next neighbours nudged him. Child as he was, he was desperate with hunger, and reckless with misery. He rose from the table; and advancing to the master, basin and spoon in hand, said: somewhat alarmed at his own temerity:

"Please, Sir, I want some more."

The master was a fat, healthy man; but he turned very pale. He gazed in stupefied astonishment on the small rebel for some seconds, and then clung for support to the copper. The assistants were paralysed with wonder; the boys with fear.

"What!" said the master at length, in a faint voice.

"Please, Sir," replied Oliver, "I want some more."

The master aimed a blow at Oliver's head with the ladle; pinioned him in his arms; and shrieked aloud for the beadle.

The board were sitting in solemn conclave, when Mr.

Bumble rushed into the room in great excitement, and addressing the gentleman in the high chair, said,

"Mr. Limbkins, I beg your pardon, Sir! Oliver Twist has asked for more!"

There was a general start. Horror was depicted on every countenance.

"For *more!*" said Mr. Limbkins. "Compose yourself, Bumble, and answer me distinctly. Do I understand that he asked for more, after he had eaten the supper allotted by the dietary?"

"He did, Sir," replied Bumble.

"That boy will be hung," said the gentleman in the white waistcoat. "I know that boy will be hung."

Nobody controverted the prophetic gentleman's opinion. An animated discussion took place. Oliver was ordered into instant confinement; and a bill was next morning pasted on the outside of the gate, offering a reward of five pounds to anybody who would take Oliver Twist off the hands of the parish. In other words, five pounds and Oliver Twist were offered to any man or woman who wanted an apprentice to any trade, business, or calling.

"I never was more convinced of anything in my life," said the gentleman in the white waistcoat.

Christopher Marlowe, from Doctor Faustus

Faustus. Ah, Faustus,
Now hast thou but one bare hour to live,
And then thou must be damn'd perpetually!
Stand still, you ever-moving spheres of heaven,
That time may cease, and midnight never come;
Fair Nature's eye, rise, rise again, and make
Perpetual day; or let this hour be but
A year, a month, a week, a natural day,
That Faustus may repent and save his soul!
O lente, lente currite, noctis equi!
The stars move still, time runs, the clock will strike,

The devil will come, and Faustus must be damn'd.
O, I'll leap up to my God!—Who pulls me down?—
See, see, where Christ's blood streams in the firmament!
One drop would save my soul, half a drop: ah, my Christ!
Ah, rend not my heart for naming of my Christ!
Yet will I call on him: O spare me, Lucifer!—
Where is it now? 'tis gone: and see, where God
Stretcheth out his arm, and bends his ireful brows!
Mountains and hills, come, come and fall on me,
And hide me from the heavy wrath of God!
No, no!
Then will I headlong run unto the earth:
Earth, gape! O, no, it will not harbour me!
You stars that reign'd at my nativity,
Whose influence hath allotted death and hell,
Now draw up Faustus, like a foggy mist,
Into the entrails of yon labouring clouds,
That, when you vomit forth into the air,
My limbs may issue from your smoky mouths,
So that my soul may but ascend to heaven!

(*The clock strikes the half-hour*)

Ah, half the hour is past! 'twill all be past anon,
O God,
If thou wilt not have mercy on my soul,
Yet for Christ's sake, whose blood hath ransom'd me,
Impose some end to my incessant pain;
Let Faustus live in hell a thousand years,
A hundred thousand, and at last be sav'd!
O, no end is limited to damnèd souls!
Why wert thou not a creature wanting soul?
Or why is this immortal that thou hast?
Ah, Pythagoras' metempsychosis, were that true,
This soul should fly from me, and I be chang'd
Unto some brutish beast! all beasts are happy,
For, when they die,
Their souls are soon dissolv'd in elements;
But mine must live still to be plagu'd in hell.
Curs'd be the parents that engender'd me!
No, Faustus, curse thyself, curse Lucifer

That hath depriv'd thee of the joys of heaven.

(The clock strikes twelve)

O, it strikes, it strikes! Now, body, turn to air,
Or Lucifer will bear thee quick to hell!

(Thunder and lightning)

O soul, be chang'd into little water-drops,
And fall into the ocean, ne'er be found!

Enter Devils

My God, my God, look not so fierce on me!
Adders and serpents, let me breathe a while!
Ugly hell, gape not! come not, Lucifer!
I'll burn my books!—Ah, Mephistophilis!

(Exeunt Devils *with* Faustus)

Henry David Thoreau, from "On Civil Disobedience"

I have paid no poll-tax for six years. I was put into a jail once on this account, for one night; and, as I stood considering the walls of solid stone, two or three feet thick, the door of wood and iron, a foot thick, and the iron grating which strained the light, I could not help being struck with the foolishness of that institution which treated me as if I were mere flesh and blood and bones, to be locked up. I wondered that it should have concluded at length that this was the best use it could put me to, and had never thought to avail itself of my services in some way. I saw that, if there was a wall of stone between me and my townsmen, there was a still more difficult one to climb or break through, before they could get to be as free as I was. I did not for a moment feel confined, and the walls seemed a great waste of stone and mortar. I felt as if I alone of all my townsmen had paid my tax. They plainly did not know how to treat me, but behaved like persons who are underbred. In every threat and in every compliment there was a blunder; for they thought that my chief desire was to stand the other side of that stone wall. I could not but smile to see how industriously they locked the door on my meditations, which followed them out again without let or hinderance, and *they* were really all that was dangerous. As they could not reach me, they had resolved to punish my body; just as boys, if they cannot come at some person against whom they have a spite, will abuse his dog. I saw that the State was half-witted, that it was timid as a lone woman with her silver spoons, and that it did not know its friends from its foes, and I lost all my remaining respect for it, and pitied it.

Thus the State never intentionally confronts a man's sense, intellectual or moral, but only his body, his senses. It is not armed with superior wit or honesty, but with superior physical strength. I was not born to be forced. I will breathe after my own fashion. Let us see who is the strongest. What force has a multitude? They only can force me who obey a higher law than I. They force me to become like themselves. I do not hear of *men* being *forced* to live this way or that by masses of men. What sort of life were that to live? When I meet a government which says to me, "Your money or your life," why should I be in haste to give it my money? It may be in a great strait, and not know what to do: I cannot help that. It must help itself; do as I do. It is not worth the while to snivel about it. I am not responsible for the successful working of the machinery of society.

Walt Whitman, from "Out of the Cradle Endlessly Rocking"

Out of the cradle endlessly rocking,
Out of the mocking-bird's throat, the musical shuttle,
Out of the Ninth-month midnight,
Over the sterile sands and the fields beyond, where the
    child leaving his bed wander'd alone, bareheaded,
    barefoot,
Down from the shower'd halo,
Up from the mystic play of shadows twining and twist-
    ing as if they were alive,

Out from the patches of briers and blackberries,
From the memories of the bird that chanted to me,
From your memories sad brother, from the fitful risings
    and fallings I heard,
From under that yellow half-moon late-risen and swollen
    as if with tears,
From those beginning notes of yearning and love there
    in the mist,
From the thousand responses of my heart never to cease,
From the myriad thence-arous'd words,
From the word stronger and more delicious than any,
For such as now they start the scene revisiting,
As a flock, twittering, rising, or overhead passing,
Borne hither, ere all eludes me, hurriedly,
A man, yet by these tears a little boy again,
Throwing myself on the sand, confronting the waves,
I, chanter of pains and joys, uniter of here and hereafter,
Taking all hints to use them, but swiftly leaping beyond
    them,
A reminiscence sing.

Once Paumanok,
When the lilac-scent was in the air and Fifth-month
    grass was growing,
Up this seashore in some briers,
Two feather'd guests from Alabama, two together,
And their nest, and four light-green eggs spotted with
    brown,
And every day the he-bird to and fro near at hand,
And every day the she-bird crouch'd on her nest, silent,
    with bright eyes,
And every day I, a curious boy, never too close, never
    disturbing them,
Cautiously peering, absorbing, translating.

Shine! shine! shine!
Pour down your warmth, great sun!
While we bask, we two together.

Two together!
Winds blow south, or winds blow north,
Day come white, or night come black,
Home, or rivers and mountains from home,
Singing all time, minding no time,
While we two keep together.
Till of a sudden,
May-be kill'd, unknown to her mate,
One forenoon the she-bird crouch'd not on the nest,
Nor return'd that afternoon, nor the next,
Nor ever appear'd again.

And thenceforward all summer in the sound of the sea,
And at night under the full of the moon in calmer
    weather,
Over the hoarse surging of the sea,
Or flitting from brier to brier by day,
I saw, I heard at intervals the remaining one, the he-bird,
The solitary guest from Alabama.

Blow! blow! blow!
Blow up sea-winds along Paumanok's shore;
I wait and I wait till you blow my mate to me.

Yes, when the stars glisten'd,
All night long on the prong of a moss-scallop'd stake,
Down almost amid the slapping waves,
Sat the lone singer wonderful causing tears.

He call'd on his mate,
He pour'd forth the meanings which I of all men know.
Yes my brother I know,
The rest might not, but I have treasur'd every note,
For more than once dimly down to the beach gliding,
Silent, avoiding the moonbeams, blending myself with
    the shadows,
Recalling now the obscure shapes, the echoes, the sounds
    and sights after their sorts,
The white arms out in the breakers tirelessly tossing,

I, with bare feet, a child, the wind wafting my hair,
Listen'd long and long.

Listen'd to keep, to sing, now translating the notes,
Following you my brother.

Charles Dickens, from Great Expectations

"Hold your noise!" cried a terrible voice, as a man started up from among the graves at the side of the church porch. "Keep still, you little devil, or I'll cut your throat!"

A fearful man, all in coarse grey, with a great iron on his leg. A man with no hat, and with broken shoes, and with an old rag tied round his head. A man who had been soaked in water, and smothered in mud, and lamed by stones, and cut by flints, and stung by nettles, and torn by briars; who limped, and shivered, and glared and growled; and whose teeth chattered in his head as he seized me by the chin.

"O! Don't cut my throat, sir," I pleaded in terror. "Pray don't do it, sir."

"Tell us your name!" said the man. "Quick!"

"Pip, sir."

"Once more," said the man, staring at me. "Give it mouth!"

"Pip. Pip, sir."

"Show us where you live," said the man. "Pint out the place!"

I pointed to where our village lay, on the flat in-shore among the alder-trees and pollards, a mile or more from the church.

The man, after looking at me for a moment, turned me upside down, and emptied my pockets. There was nothing in them but a piece of bread. When the church came to itself—for he was so sudden and strong that he made it go head over heels before me, and I saw the steeple under my feet—when the church came to itself, I say, I was seated on a high tombstone, trembling, while he ate the bread ravenously.

"You young dog," said the man, licking his lips, "what fat cheeks you ha' got."

I believe they were fat, though I was at that time under-sized, for my years, and not strong.

"Darn Me if I couldn't eat 'em," said the man, with a threatening shake of his head, "and if I han't half a mind to't!"

I earnestly expressed my hope that he wouldn't, and held tighter to the tombstone on which he had put me; partly, to keep myself upon it; partly, to keep myself from crying.

"Now lookee here!" said the man. "Where's your mother?"

"There, sir!" said I.

He started, made a short run, and stopped and looked over his shoulder.

"There, sir!" I timidly explained. "Also Georgiana. That's my mother."

"Oh!" said he, coming back. "And is that your father alonger your mother?"

"Yes, sir," said I; "him too; late of this parish."

"Ha!" he muttered then, considering. "Who d'ye live with—supposin' you're kindly let to live, which I han't made up my mind about?"

"My sister, sir—Mrs. Joe Gargery—wife of Joe Gargery, the blacksmith, sir."

"Blacksmith, eh?" said he. And looked down at his leg.

After darkly looking at his leg and at me several times, he came closer to my tombstone, took me by both arms, and tilted me back as far as he could hold me; so that his eyes looked most powerfully down into mine, and mine looked most helplessly up into his.

"Now lookee here," he said, "the question being whether you're to be let to live. You know what a file is?"

"Yes, sir."

"And you know what wittles is?"

"Yes, sir."

After each question he tilted me over a little more, so as to give me a greater sense of helplessness and danger.

"You get me a file." He tilted me again. "And you get me wittles." He tilted me again. "You bring 'em both to me."

He tilted me again. "Or I'll have your heart and liver out."
He tilted me again.

I was dreadfully frightened, and so giddy that I clung to
him with both hands, and said, "If you would kindly please to
let me keep upright, sir, perhaps I shouldn't be sick, and perhaps I could attend more."

He gave me a most tremendous dip and roll, so that the
church jumped over its own weather-cock. Then, he held me
by the arms in an upright position on the top of the stone, and
went on in these fearful terms:

"You bring me, to-morrow morning early, that file and
them wittles. You bring the lot to me, at that old Battery over
yonder. You do it, and you never dare to say a word or dare to
make a sign concerning your having seen such a person as me,
or any person sumever, and you shall be let to live. You fail,
or you go from my words in any partickler, no matter how
small it is, and your heart and your liver shall be tore out,
roasted and ate. Now, I ain't alone, as you may think I am.
There's a young man hid with me, in comparison with which
young man I am a Angel. That young man hears the words I
speak. That young man has a secret way pecooliar to himself,
of getting at a boy, and at his heart, and at his liver. It is in
wain for a boy to attempt to hide himself from that young
man. A boy may lock his door, may be warm in bed, may tuck
himself up, may draw the clothes over his head, may think
himself comfortable and safe, but that young man will softly
creep and creep his way to him and tear him open. I am a
keeping that young man from harming of you at the present
moment, with great difficulty. I find it wery hard to hold that
young man off of your inside. Now, what do you say?"

I said that I would get him the file, and I would get him
what broken bits of food I could, and I would come to him at
the Battery, early in the morning.

"Say, Lord strike you dead if you don't!" said the man.
I said so, and he took me down.

"Now," he pursued, "you remember what you've under-
took, and you remember that young man, and you get home!"

"Goo-good night, sir," I faltered.

STORIES FOR ORAL INTERPRETATION

The following stories offer an ideal opportunity to practice oral interpretation. To interpret them properly you will need to use a wide range of pitch, changes in volume, rate, and the use of pauses. Mark these elements clearly in your text. Proper preparation should leave nothing to chance, so don't try to wing it. Know what you want to do, and do it consistently every time. Knowing that you are adequately prepared will also increase your self-confidence.

Never use a tongue-in-cheek attitude on the folk tales, which have come to be considered children's literature. They are an important part of the literary heritage of the Western world.

By all means try out your interpretations on children, but be forewarned: they will inevitably seek you out for more!

The Story of the Three Bears

Once upon a time there were three bears, who lived together in a house of their own in a wood. One of them was a little, small, wee bear, and one was a middle-sized bear, and the other was a great, huge bear. They had each a pot for their porridge; a little pot for the little, small, wee bear, a middle-sized pot for the middle bear, and a great pot for the great, huge bear. And they had each a chair to sit in; a little chair for the little, small, wee bear, a middle-sized chair for the middle bear, and a great chair for the great, huge bear. And they had each a bed to sleep in; a little bed for the little, small, wee bear, a middle-sized bed for the middle bear, and a great bed for the great, huge bear.

One day, after they had made the porridge for their breakfast and poured it into their porridge pots, they walked out into the wood while the porridge was cooling, that they might not burn their mouths by beginning too soon to eat it. And while they were walking a little old woman came to the house. She could not have been a good, honest old woman;

for first she looked in at the window and then she peeped in at the keyhole; and seeing nobody in the house she lifted the latch. The door was not fastened, because the bears were good bears who did nobody any harm and never suspected that anybody would harm them. So the little old woman opened the door and went in; and well pleased she was when she saw the porridge on the table. If she had been a good little old woman she would have waited till the bears came home, and then, perhaps, they would have asked her to breakfast; for they were good bears—a little rough or so, as the manner of bears is, but for all that very good-natured and hospitable. But she was an impudent, bad old woman and set about helping herself.

So first she tasted the porridge of the great, huge bear, and that was too hot for her; and she said a bad word about that. And then she tasted the porridge of the middle bear, and that was too cold for her; and she said a bad word about that too. And then she went to the porridge of the little, small, wee bear, and tasted that, and that was neither too hot nor too cold, but just right; and she liked it so well that she ate it all up. But the naughty old woman said a bad word about the little porridge pot, because it did not hold enough for her.

Then the little old woman sat down in the chair of the great huge bear, and that was too hard for her. And then she sat down in the chair of the middle bear, and that was too soft for her. And then she sat down in the chair of the little, small, wee bear, and that was neither too hard nor too soft, but just right. So she seated herself in it, and there she sat till the bottom of the chair came out, and down came she, plump upon the ground. And the naughty old woman said a wicked word about that too.

Then the little old woman went upstairs into the bedchamber in which the three bears slept. And first she lay down upon the bed of the great, huge bear; but that was too high at the head for her. And next she lay down upon the bed of the middle bear; and that was too high at the foot for her. And then she lay down upon the bed of the little, small, wee bear; and that was neither too high at the head nor at the foot, but just right. So she covered herself up comfortably and lay there till she fell fast asleep.

By this time the three bears thought their porridge would be cool enough, so they came home to breakfast. Now, the little old woman had left the spoon of the great, huge bear standing in his porridge.

"SOMEBODY HAS BEEN AT MY PORRIDGE!"

said the great, huge bear in his great, rough, gruff voice. And when the middle bear looked at his, he saw that the spoon was standing in it too. They were wooden spoons; if they had been silver ones the naughty old woman would have put them in her pocket.

"SOMEBODY HAS BEEN AT MY PORRIDGE!"

said the middle bear in his middle voice.

Then the little, small, wee bear looked at his, and there was the spoon in the porridge pot, but the porridge was all gone.

"Somebody has been at my porridge, and has eaten it all up!"

said the little, small, wee bear in his little, small, wee voice.

Upon this the three bears, seeing that someone had entered their house and eaten up the little, small, wee bear's breakfast, began to look about them. Now, the little old woman had not put the hard cushion straight when she rose from the chair of the great, huge bear.

"SOMEBODY HAS BEEN SITTING IN MY CHAIR!"

said the great, huge bear in his great, rough, gruff voice.

And the little old woman had squatted down the soft cushion of the middle bear.

"SOMEBODY HAS BEEN SITTING IN MY CHAIR!"

said the middle bear in his middle voice.

And you know what the little old woman had done to the third chair.

*"Somebody has been sitting in my chair and has sat the bottom
of it out!"*

said the little, small, wee bear in his little, small, wee voice.

And the little old woman had pulled the bolster of the huge
bear out of its place.

"SOMEBODY HAS BEEN LYING IN MY BED!"

said the great, huge bear in his great, rough, gruff, voice.

And the little old woman had pulled the bolster of the
middle bear out of its place.

"SOMEBODY HAS BEEN LYING IN MY BED!"

said the middle bear in his middle voice.

And when the little, small, wee bear came to look at his
bed, there was the bolster in its place and the pillow in its
place upon the bolster, and upon the pillow was the little old
woman's ugly, dirty head—which was not in its place, for she
had no business there.

"Somebody has been lying in my bed—and here she is!"

said the little, small, wee bear in his little, small, wee voice.

The little old woman had heard in her sleep the great,
rough, gruff voice of the great, huge bear; but she was so fast
asleep that it was no more to her than the roaring of wind or
the rumbling of thunder. And she had heard the middle voice
of the middle bear; but it was only as if she had heard someone speaking in a dream. But when she heard the little, small,
wee voice of the little, small, wee bear, it was so sharp and so
shrill that it awakened her at once. Up she started, and when
she saw the three bears on one side of the bed she tumbled
herself out at the other and ran to the window. Now, the
window was open, because the bears, like good, tidy bears as
they were, always opened their bedchamber window when they
got up in the morning. Out the little old woman jumped; and

whether she broke her neck in the fall or ran into the wood and was lost there, or found her way out of the wood and was taken up by the constable and sent to the House of Correction for a vagrant as she was, I cannot tell. But the three bears never saw anything more of her.

Rumpelstiltzkin

There was once upon a time a poor miller who had a very beautiful daughter. Now it happened one day that he had an audience with the King, and in order to appear a person of some importance he told him that he had a daughter who could spin straw into gold. "Now that's a talent worth having," said the King to the miller. "If your daughter is as clever as you say, bring her to my palace tomorrow, and I'll put her to the test." When the girl was brought to him he led her into a room full of straw, gave her a spinning wheel and spindle, and said: "Now set to work and spin all night till early dawn, and if by that time you haven't spun the straw into gold you shall die." Then he closed the door behind him and left her alone inside.

So the poor miller's daughter sat down, and didn't know what in the world she was to do. She hadn't the least idea of how to spin straw into gold, and became at last so miserable that she began to cry. Suddenly the door opened, and in stepped a tiny little man and said: "Good evening, Miss Miller-maid; why are you crying so bitterly?" "Oh!" answered the girl, "I have to spin straw into gold, and haven't a notion how it's done." "What will you give me if I spin it for you?" asked the manikin. "My necklace," replied the girl. The little man took the necklace, sat himself down at the wheel, and whir, whir, whir, the wheel went round three times, and the bobbin was full. Then he put on another, and whir, whir, whir, the wheel went round three times, and the second too was full; and so it went on till the morning, when all the straw was spun away, and all the bobbins were full of gold. As soon as the sun rose the King came, and when he perceived the gold he was astonished and delighted, but his heart only lusted more than ever after the precious metal. He had the miller's daughter put into another room full of straw, much bigger than the first, and bade her, if she valued her life, spin it all into gold before the following morning. The girl didn't know what to do, and began to cry; then the door opened as before, and the tiny little man appeared and said: "What'll you give me if I spin the straw into gold for you?" "The ring from my finger," answered the girl. The manikin took the ring, and whir! round went the spinning wheel again, and when morning broke he had spun all the straw into glittering gold. The King was pleased beyond measure at the sight, but his greed for gold was still not satisfied, and he had the miller's daughter brought into a yet bigger room full of straw, and said: "You must spin all this away in the night; but if you succeed this time you shall become my wife." "She's only a miller's daughter, it's true," he thought; "but I couldn't find a richer wife if I were to search the whole world over." When the girl was alone the little man appeared for the third time, and said: "What'll you give me if I spin the straw for you once again?" "I've nothing more to give," answered the girl. "Then promise me when you are Queen to give me your first child." "Who knows what may not happen before that?" thought the miller's daughter; and besides, she saw no other way out of it, so she promised the manikin what he demanded, and he set to work once more and spun the straw into gold. When the King came in the morning, and found everything as he had desired, he straightway made her his wife, and the miller's daughter became a queen.

When a year had passed a beautiful son was born to her, and she thought no more of the little man, till all of a sudden one day he stepped into her room and said: "Now give me what you promised." The Queen was in a great state, and offered the little man all the riches in her kingdom if he would only leave her the child. But the manikin said: "No, a living creature is dearer to me than all the treasures in the world." Then the Queen began to cry and sob so bitterly that the little man was sorry for her, and said: "I'll give you three days to guess my name, and if you find it out in that time, you may keep your child."

Then the Queen pondered the whole night over all the names she had ever heard, and sent a messenger to scour the land, and to pick up far and near any names he could come across. When the little man arrived on the following day she began with Kasper, Melchior, Belshazzar, and all the other names she knew, in a string, but at each one the manikin called out: "That's not my name." The next day she sent to inquire the names of all the people in the neighborhood, and had a long list of the most uncommon and extraordinary for the little man when he made his appearance. "Is your name, perhaps, Sheepshanks, Cruickshanks, Spindleshanks?" But he always replied: "That's not my name." On the third day the messenger returned and announced: "I have not been able to find any new names, but as I came upon a high hill round the corner of the wood, where the foxes and hares bid each other good night, I saw a little house, and in front of the house burned a fire, and round the fire sprang the most grotesque little man, hopping on one leg and crying:

"Tomorrow I brew, today I bake,
And then the child away I'll take;
For little deems my royal dame
That Rumpelstiltzkin is my name!"

You may imagine the Queen's delight at hearing the name, and when the little man stepped in shortly afterward and asked: "Now, my lady Queen, what's my name?" she asked first: "Is your name Conrad?" "No." "Is your name Harry?" "No." "Is your name, perhaps, Rumpelstiltzkin?" "Some demon has told you that! Some demon has told you that!" screamed the little man, and in his rage drove his right foot so far into the ground that it sank in up to his waist; then in a passion he seized the left foot with both hands and tore himself in two.

Little Red Riding-Hood

Once upon a time there lived in a certain village a little country girl, the prettiest creature ever seen. Her mother was excessively fond of her; and her grandmother doted on her still more. This good woman had made for her a little red riding-hood; which became the girl so extremely well that everybody called her Little Red Riding-Hood.

One day her mother, having made some custards, said to her:

"Go, my dear, and see how thy grandmamma does, for I hear she has been very ill; carry her a custard, and this little pot of butter."

Little Red Riding-Hood set out immediately to go to her grandmother, who lived in another village.

As she was going through the wood, she met with Gaffer Wolf, who had a very great mind to eat her up, but he dared not, because of some faggot-makers hard by in the forest. He asked her whither she was going. The poor child, who did not know that it was dangerous to stay and hear a wolf talk, said to him:

"I am going to see my grandmamma and carry her a custard and a little pot of butter from my mamma."

"Does she live far off?" said the wolf.

"Oh! Ay," answered Little Red Riding-Hood. "It is beyond that mill you see there, at the first house in the village."

"Well," said the wolf, "and I'll go and see her too. I'll go this way and you go that, and we shall see who will be there soonest."

The wolf began to run as fast as he could, taking the nearest way, and the little girl went by that farthest about, diverting herself in gathering nuts, running after butterflies, and making nosegays of such little flowers as she met with. The wolf was not long before he got to the old woman's house. He knocked at the door—tap, tap.

"Who's there?"

"Your grandchild, Little Red Riding-Hood," replied the wolf, counterfeiting her voice; "who has brought you a custard and a little pot of butter sent you by Mamma."

The good grandmother, who was in bed, because she was somewhat ill, cried out:

"Pull the bobbin, and the latch will go up."

The wolf pulled the bobbin, and the door opened, and

then presently he fell upon the good woman and ate her up in a moment, for it was more than three days since he had touched a bite. He then shut the door and went into the grandmother's bed, expecting Little Red Riding-Hood, who came some time afterward and knocked at the door—tap, tap.

"Who's there?"

Little Red Riding-Hood, hearing the big voice of the wolf, was at first afraid; but, believing her grandmother had got a cold and was hoarse, answered:

" 'Tis your grandchild, Little Red Riding-Hood, who has brought you a custard and a little pot of butter Mamma sends you."

The wolf cried out to her, softening his voice as much as he could:

"Pull the bobbin, and the latch will go up."

Little Red Riding Hood pulled the bobbin, and the door opened.

The wolf, seeing her come in, said to her, hiding himself under the bedclothes:

"Put the custard and the little pot of butter upon the stool, and come and lie down with me."

Little Red Riding-Hood undressed herself and went into bed, where, being greatly amazed to see how her grandmother looked in her night clothes, she said to her:

"Grandmamma, what great arms you have got!"

"That is the better to hug thee, my dear."

"Grandmamma, what great legs you have got!"

"That is to run the better, my child."

"Grandmamma, what great ears you have got!"

"That is to hear the better, my child."

"Grandmamma, what great eyes you have got!"

"It is to see the better, my child."

"Grandmamma, what great teeth you have got!"

"That is to eat thee up."

And, saying these words, this wicked wolf fell upon Little Red Riding-Hood, and ate her all up.

15

Steps Toward Speech-Making

*W*e have considered the preparation of the voice as an instrument. Let us assume you are now ready to make a speech of your own. First, pick a subject in which you are interested and about which you feel some enthusiasm. If *you* are not enthusiastic about your subject, your audience will never be.

PARTS OF A GOOD SPEECH

A good speech is divided into three parts: *introduction, body,* and *conclusion.* The introduction is not easy to write. Too many speakers are happy to take the first available sentence, thinking, "This will do!" But a good introduction must have an element of surprise in it, something that attracts the listener's attention while it incorporates the main idea of the speech.

Picture an oak-panelled classroom in an Ivy League men's

251

college on the first day of classes in September. A warm breeze blows through the windows, the smell of furniture polish from the well-kept room blends with the smell of the newly cut grass, and an expectant class awaits a tardy unknown, a new speech professor. Finally the professor slowly enters the room. All eyes are upon him as he mounts the steps to the massive podium and without speaking sweeps the class with his eyes. Then he solemnly spits on the podium. Taking a clean handkerchief from his pocket he slowly proceeds to wipe the podium clean, saying, "My name is Professor John Smith, and you will never forget it as long as you live!"

"He was right," a witness to the above scene told me. "I'll never forget that moment."

The clever professor went on to explain to his class the importance of a good introduction. It is true that in his example he did not incorporate the main body of his course; but he did a splendid job of grasping his audience's attention. He used the pause, the principle of eye contact, and an attention-getting introduction.

Suppose you were going to make a speech dealing with the defeat of a bill to make college tuition tax deductible. You say: "Last week in Washington, D.C., a bill that would have made it possible for us to use college tuition as a tax deduction was defeated."

But the same introduction, much improved, might go: "Last week in Washington, D.C., each person in this room lost thousands of dollars."

The second introduction almost ensures the personal involvement of your listeners.

The body of your speech is dependent on the facts you include. Use the library to get historical facts, scientific facts, quotations from authorities, examples and illustrations, statistical evidence, graphs, charts, pictures. These are the materials from which you build your speech, but use them wisely. Avoid overwhelming your audience with a deluge of undigested facts. Do not use prejudiced authorities, and when you do introduce an authority, give a thumbnail biography. Not, "Mr. Smith says . . . ," but, "Mr. Smith, President of —— College, assistant to the President on —— Committee, author of ——, says . . . ."

Finally, the conclusion of your speech, once the evidence is presented, should briefly repeat and restate the main idea that you presented in your introduction.

TAILORING YOUR SPEECH

Your speech must be tailored to fit a variety of specifications.

First, the beginning speaker tends to cover too much territory. Limit your subject and always tailor it to the assigned time. Too often a speaker given a limit of three, five, or ten minutes complains when he is cut off at fifteen that he was just getting warmed to his subject, as though it were someone else's fault.

Tailor your speech to a listening, not a reading, audience. Remember that there is a difference between written and oral style. If your speech were being read, the reader could refer back at leisure to a point on a previous page. As it is being delivered orally, you must make your ideas clear the first time. Use statistics, quotations, and above all examples, and make the examples vivid. Keep your vocabulary lean and sharp; avoid polysyllabic words.

Tailor your speech to the specific audience. Are you addressing the DAR or the Steelworkers' Union? If you are speaking as a specialist, be careful not to delve too deep into your subject unless your audience is made up of fellow specialists.

Tailor your speech to the place. One cold, rainy night I went to hear a celebrated speaker. The hall was appallingly deserted, but a few scattered persons in wet raincoats waited patiently. When he appeared he quickly overcame his hurt vanity. Adjusting to the situation, he warmly invited the scattered audience to "come on down front and get together!" This saved the evening, for the huge hall no longer seemed so big and empty when the few listeners gathered into a staunch group of over a hundred.

Tailor your speech also to whatever goes on in the room

where you are speaking. A baby cries; someone faints and has to be carried out; someone has a coughing fit; latecomers march right down the center aisle to the front row. A beginning speaker, mesmerized by his own performance, might ignore the baby, the body, the cough, the latecomers, and go doggedly on, competing at losing odds with a rival production. Instead, stare at the crying baby until it is taken out of the room, wait respectfully for the body to be carried out, the cougher to subside or leave, the latecomers to take their seats—then go on with your talk. Be in control and aware of your speaking environment.

As you speak you will be more natural if you think of the occasion not as an ordeal, but as a conversation. Imagine that you are alone in a room, then a friend joins you and you begin to relate an experience. Another friend joins you, and another, and so on, as you continue conversation, widening it to include all those present. A good speaker is one who can make his audience feel this personal element. You can make each listener feel that you are speaking to him individually.

To increase this effect, use eye contact. Sweep the room with your eyes, turning your head slowly so that you take in everyone's eyes.

I once had a student who kept his eyes riveted to my necktie when he spoke to me. When he addressed the class, he refused to look at any member of the audience. When I pointed this out to him one day, he flooded me with past experiences that proved he was perfectly aware of his bad habit. "My boss thought I must be a crook because I never looked him in the eye! . . . I could never get a girl to believe I was sincere!" and so on. We worked on his problem, and by the end of the term he was able to look a person squarely in the eye. The improvement was immense. No one can even be properly introduced, let alone make a speech, without making eye contact.

PREPARING FOR DELIVERY

The beginning speaker has a problem of attachment to his manuscript and tends to do a straight job of reading, feeling that without his script he will be lost. But reading a script can prevent eye contact and rob one of spontaneity. It is better to work spontaneously from a good outline. A great many students are reluctant to use outlines, but college work demands the constant distillation of chapters into essential ideas. To make a good speech take the following course:

1. Gather your facts and materials from the library.
2. Organize your material.
3. Write a rough draft of your speech.
4. From this make your outline, writing it on small, three-by-five-inch cards.
5. Practice delivering the speech from the outline. Remember that the outline is composed of ideas and is the skeleton of your speech. Destroy the manuscript after the outline is prepared, lest you fall into the trap of memorizing or reading.

Memorizing

Memory work is not necessary in speech preparation. It is a waste of energy and a dangerous practice. It is paralyzing for a student to stand and with a glazed eye read off a speech from the teleprompter of his memory. The impression of conversational spontaneity is completely gone.

Have faith that words will come to you when you prepare from an outline. As a matter of fact, if you will practice orally five or ten times from an outline marked for emphasis, pauses, changes in volume and rate, you will discover that the same words will come to you automatically, but in a fresh and spontaneous manner, because your ideas are meaningful to you and are charged with significant emotions. Remember that no matter how meritorious a speech is in content, it is its delivery that will be responsible for its ultimate success.

Rehearsal

One last frequent worry on the part of students is expressed by, "What should I do with my *hands?*"

Here is one of the few absolute dicta in connection with speech-making. Never, never use a mirror to practice attitudes. Why? You are in danger of developing a narcissistic relationship with yourself that will prevent communication with the audience. You must forget yourself in order to project your ideas. If you have watched yourself in a mirror, you will stand there and your mind will flash messages that can only short-circuit you as a speaker: "Do I look as good as I did in front of the mirror?" "Is my tie straight?" "How's my eye makeup?" Or worse, "Here's where I raise my right hand in a fist—will it look as good as it did at home?" Beware of the mirror and the paralysis of self-consciousness.

Next, beware of the planned, mechanical gesture. In the nineteenth century, teachers of the popular contemporary art of oratory had elaborate rules for the appropriate gesture. Henry Ward Beecher, a preacher of such charm and force that he was the superstar of his age (with special Sunday excursion boats run to his Brooklyn church), practiced voice exercises and gestures in the woods until he had achieved perfection—according to the standards of his time. I am certain that if we could hear Beecher's voice and judge it for range and tone it would score phenomenally. But if we were to watch him deliver a speech, we would be embarrassed by his flamboyancy of gesture and delivery, and would have to suppress laughter.

When Beecher preached, each emotion had its gesture so that in time, by a literal shorthand, each gesture conveyed an emotion. But all that has long gone out of style.

What is the proper approach to gesture today? Use common sense, restraint and simplicity, and good taste. Stand relaxed. You should now know how to relax. Leave your hands alone, either at your side or gently holding the podium. Do not attempt to hold large sheets of paper in your hands; they will rattle as certainly as a teacup will rattle on the saucer in a nervous actor's fingers. If you work correctly, your feelings and emotions in your relaxed body will create certain spontaneous gestures that will be "right." Concentrate on preparing your speech so that you know what emotions you want to project. Relax your body and the rest will follow.

You may ask, "What if I practice my speech and make just the right gesture once? If I remember to make it there again, is it phony?"

Don't put it in deliberately. Have the confidence to know that if it happened spontaneously once, it will again. Your response to your material, if well-studied, will be consistent. It is like a road map. The development of the ideas in your material are the roads you follow to the known conclusion. Make sure your understanding of these ideas is meaningful to you and creates a response to your feelings in your instrument (affecting volume, rate, and pitch) and your body (affecting gestures).

Avoid pounding the podium. I have seen too many physical types try to emphasize sincerity by slamming the podium with a resounding wham, following this up with a mere trickle of vocal energy. So much energy is put into the arm muscle that none is left for the diaphragm. Do not break the furniture; put the energy into your instrument. By this time you should know how, and should not have to give the podium a frustrated beating.

Finally, remember to enjoy yourself when you speak. If you are suffering, you can be certain that your audience suffers with you. Have fun and your audience will enjoy the occasion too.

Many students ask, "How can I ever be self-confident in a public-speaking situation?" The answer is simple: You will be confident when you know that you are adequately prepared. Develop your instrument and prepare your material and you will be equal to any speaking challenge.

SAMPLE SPEECHES

The following speeches of Clarence Darrow, famous trial lawyer and brilliant speaker, are excellent examples for the speech student. Read both speeches over two or three times. Then decide on delivery and see how well you can do. Mark your text for pitch, volume, rate, pauses.

Clarence Darrow, A lecture on John Brown

On the seventeenth of October, 1859, about eight o'clock at night, the little army left the farmhouse for Harpers Ferry, five miles away. They quickly captured the arsenal and took possession of the town. Then their plans began to go awry; the citizens rallied; the regular troops were brought upon the scene; Brown and his followers were penned in the engine house, and made a last desperate stand against overwhelming odds. John Brown was seriously wounded, two of his sons were shot down by his side, six escaped, all the rest were either shot or hanged.

Brown was indicted, immediately placed on trial while still suffering from his wounds, was brought in and out of the courthouse on a cot. Of course, [he was] convicted, and within six weeks after the raid, was hanged. He was convicted and hanged. For though one of the purest and bravest and highest-minded patriots of any age, he was tried by the law; the law which makes no account of the motives of men, but decides upon their deeds alone.

The news of John Brown's raid sent an electric shock around the world; the slave power was aghast at the audacity of the act, and knew not where to turn. The leading abolitionists of the North were stunned and terrified at the manhunt coming on. The great William Lloyd Garrison promptly and fiercely denounced Brown's mad act. Beecher and Seward cried out against the man who had so criminally and recklessly hazarded his friends and the cause. Bold and wrathful were all these old abolitionists when there was no risk to run, but here was a maniac who transformed their words to deeds.

In the first mad days but one man stood fearless and unmoved while the universe was falling around his head, and this man was John Brown. When faint voices cried out for his rescue, Brown promptly made reply, "I do not know that I ought to encourage any attempt to save my life; I think I cannot now better serve the cause I love than to die for it, and in my death, I may do more than in my life."

But soon the mad frenzy of the mob began to die away. A few brave souls stood unmoved in the fury of the storm. While Brown still lived, the calm, sane voice of Emerson called his countrymen to view Brown's deeds in the light of the motives that fired his soul; he told the world that soon the day would come when his deeds with their motives would place John Brown among the martyrs and the heroes of the earth. Theodore Parker did not lose his head in the mad unseemly haste to save his neck, and brave old Wendell Phillips fearlessly hurled his maledictions in the teeth of the maddened and exultant foe. But when the scaffold bore its fruit, and the dead hero's heart was cold, the pulse of humanity once more began to beat; the timid, the coward, the time server, the helpless and the weak looked on the brave, cold clay, and from a million throats a cry for vengeance was lifted to the stars. Men cried from the hustings to wake a sleeping world; newspapers condemned the act; ministers who still were Christians appealed from the judgment of the court to the judgment of their God; church bells with sad tones tolled out the tidings of Brown's passing soul, and men and angels wept above his bier. And still the tide rolled on, until in less than two short years the land resounded with the call to arms, and millions of men were hurrying to the field of strife to complete the work John Brown began.

Once more at Harpers Ferry was gathered a band pledged to the same great cause—"the Liberty of Man"—a band that under the leadership of Grant swept down the great Black Way with fire and sword, and in a sea of blood washed the crime of slavery away.

But while the victorious hosts were destroying the in-

famous system that had cursed the earth so long, John Brown
was sleeping in a felon's grave, and around his decaying neck
was the black mark of the hangman's noose, the reward of a
Christian world for the devoted soul that had made the
supreme sacrifice for his loyalty and love. More than any other
man, his mad raid broke the bondsman's chain. True, the
details of his plan had failed, where the plans of prophets
always fail: the men who worked with him, and the poor for
whom he fought, left him to die alone. John Brown offered
his life and the lives of those he loved for the despised and
weak; and while he fought and died, these, idle and nerveless
and stupid, looked blindly on as their masters strangled him to
death.

But this story, too, is old, old as the human race. Ever
and ever hangs the devoted Christ upon the cross, and ever
with faint heart and dumb mouths and palsied hands, the
poor for whom he toiled, stand helpless and watch their savior
die.

The world has long since accepted the results of John
Brown's work. Great as was the cost, all men know that it was
worth the price. But even now the idle, carping, and foolish
still ask, "Did Brown do right, and would it not better have
been done some other way?" Of all the foolish questions asked
by idle tongues, the most childish is to ask if a great work
should not have been done some other way. Nothing in the
universe that was ever done, could have been done in any
other way. He who accepts results must accept with them every
act that leads to the result. And all who think must accept all
results. High above the hand of man is the hand of destiny,
all potent in the world. To deny destiny is to deny God, and all
the forces that move the universe of which man is so small a
part. To condemn an act as wrong assumes that the laws of
justice laid down by the weak minds of man are the same as
the laws of the universe, which stretch over infinite matter,
infinite time and space, and regards nothing less than all.

The world may ask the question, "Did John Brown's work
fit the everlasting scheme of things?" It cannot ask whether
this or that taken apart from all, was good or bad. Nothing in
the universe stands or can stand apart from all the rest. Nature

works in a great broad way, and makes no account of the laws of justice as man has laid them down. Nature would prepare the earth for the human race; she sends a glacier plowing across a continent carrying death and destruction in its path and leaving powdered rock and fertile valleys in its wake. For some mysterious reason, she would change a portion of the globe, and she sends earthquake to cover the land with sea, to raise islands in the trackless ocean, to shake down cities, lay waste provinces, and destroy the "unjust" and the "just" alike.

John Brown was right; he was an instrument in the hands of a higher power. He acted as that power had given him the brain to see, and the will to do. In answering his inquisitors in Virginia, he said, "True, I went against the laws of man, but whether it be right to obey God or man, judge ye."

Long ago it was said, "By their fruits ye shall know them." The fruits of John Brown's life are plain for all to see; while time shall last, men and women, sons and daughters of bondsmen and slaves, will live by the light of freedom, be inspired by the hope of liberty.

The earth needs and will always need its Browns; these poor, sensitive, prophetic souls, feeling the suffering of the world, and taking its sorrows on their burdened backs. It sorely needs the prophets who look far out into the dark, and through the long and painful vigils of the night, wait for the coming day. They wait and watch, while slow and cold and halting, the morning dawns, the sun rises and waxes to the noon, and wanes to the twilight and another night comes on. The radical of today is the conservative of tomorrow, and other martyrs take up the work through other nights, and the dumb and stupid world plants its weary feet upon the slippery sand, soaked by their blood, and the world moves on.

Clarence Darrow, from debate on "Is Capital Punishment a Wise Policy?" (Negative Rebuttal)

Fifteen minutes in which to answer my friend and the chairman is, perhaps, a little short; but still I can do it.

I want to say, in spite of the chairman having the added

dignity of a chairman, that every single statement that I made is true as to the judges and the people. The long list of one hundred and seventy crimes was abolished in England because juries would not convict, until here and there, as Mr. Marshall says, some decent judges circumvented the law. For God's sake, Mr. Marshall, a great lawyer like you talking about judges circumventing the law!

Now, there is no use of mincing matters over this. There isn't any human being who ever investigated this subject that doesn't know it. Every step in humanity, in the administration of the law, has been against courts and by the people—every step. It is all right for judges to write essays about it after it has happened. But over and over again, as in New England, they instructed juries to hang old women for witchcraft, and they refused. And every clergyman stood there, urging it. But they refused, and the old women were not hanged—and that was abolished in New England.

Neither am I making a misstatement when I say that good lawyers are not appointed to defend poor clients. Now, look that up. There may be, here and there, some conspicuous case, but the run of poor clients in a court is without the help of lawyers who are fit to do it. And I will guarantee that every man waiting for death in Sing Sing is there without the aid of a good lawyer.

Now, look that up. I know about these good lawyers. They don't do it. Do you suppose you can get a member of the Bar Association to give his time for nothing? No, he leaves it to us criminal lawyers. Nothing doing—they are taking care of the wealth of corporations. That is what they are doing.

A VOICE: How about you?

MR. DARROW: You want to know about me? I have defended more than half of my clients for nothing. Ever since I began the practice of law, I have given more than a third of the time of every man in my office for nothing. If you want to know about me, that is the truth.

A VOICE: Was it by appointment?

MR. DARROW: No, I never was appointed in my life— never. No judge would take my time by appointing me, any more than they do any lawyer when he wants to get paid for his services.

Now, I am going to finish this debate.

My friend doesn't believe in heredity. I didn't suppose there was more than one man in the United States who didn't believe in heredity. I knew that Mr. Bryan didn't. Am I to enter into a discussion about the ABCs of science? There isn't a scientist on earth who doesn't believe and say that man is the product of heredity and environment alone. Of course, it takes one from the Dark Ages to believe in killing human beings.

He talks of logic. He says I don't believe in free will (I do not) and that, therefore, I would say that no man should be confined. Does that follow? No.

Why do we send people to prison? Because we want to hurt them? No. We send them in self-defense, because for some reason they can't adjust themselves to life. And no other reason than that is admissible, and no humane person believes any other reason is admissible.

Why? You want to know about it? If you do, read, study. There have been a great number of scientific men whose work has been for the benefit of the human race. A great many of these have been students of criminology. Yet, we heard them sneered at this afternoon by men who know nothing, men who dare say that heredity is all "bunk."

Well, of course, it seems kind of hopeless to teach people anything. I wonder if the gentleman believes in heredity in the breeding of cattle. I wonder if he believes in heredity in the breeding of pigs. I wonder if he believes in heredity—well, didn't he ever see any heredity in a human being? Didn't you see your mother, your father, your grandmother, your grandfather? Why discuss it? Everybody knows it. And those who don't know it, don't want to know it—that's all.

I did not say that every case in prison was that of a poor person. I said that almost all of them were. My friend said that, probably, to make the utterly absurd statement about a terrible crime—the most terrible, he said—because he read it in the newspapers. He doesn't know anything about it—but it is common for a judge to pass judgment upon things he is not acquainted with.

I said that the great mass of people in prison are the poor, Am I right or am I wrong?

Where do you live that you don't know it? I want to get you to look into this question. And you can't do it in a minute. You can sing hosannas when some poor devil is sent to Kingdom Come, but you can't understand without thought and study. And, contrary to my friend, everybody doesn't think. He says everybody born has free will. Have they? Everybody born has free will—what do you think of that?

Now, am I right in my statement that it is the poor who fill prisons and who go to the scaffold and who are prosecuted and persecuted? Nobody who knows anything about it believes that the rich are the ones, or any considerable fraction of the rich.

He hasn't given me time to shed tears over the victims of the murderers. I am as sorry for them as he is, because I hate cruelty; no matter who suffers, I hate it. I don't love it and get pleasure out of it when it is done by hanging somebody by the neck until dead—no.

But, now, let me tell you. You can find out. I will guarantee that you can go through the Tombs and you won't find one out of a thousand that isn't poor. You may go to Sing Sing and you will not find one out of a thousand who isn't poor. Since the world began, a procession of the weak and the poor and the helpless has been going to our jails and our prisons and to their deaths. They have been judged as if they were strong and rich and intelligent. They have been victims, whether punishable by death for one crime or one hundred and seventy crimes.

And, we say, this is no time to soften the human heart. Isn't it? Whenever it is the hardest, that is the best time to get at it. When is the time? If he is right, why not re-enact the penal codes of the past? What do you suppose the American Bar Association knows about this subject?

A Voice: More than you.

Mr. Darrow: Do you think so? Then you don't know what you are talking about. Their members are too busy defending corporations. There isn't a criminologist in the world that hasn't said what I have said. And you may read any history or any philosophy and they each and every one point out that after every great war in the world, wherever it was, crimes of violence increased. Do I need to prove it?

Let me ask you this: Do you think man, in any sense, is a creature of environment? Do you think you people could, day by day, wish and hope and pray for the slaughter of thousands of Germans because they were your enemies, and not become callous to suffering? Do you think that children of our schools and our Sunday schools could be taught killing and be as kindly and as tender after it as before? Do you think man does not feel every emotion that comes to him, no matter from what source it comes? Do you think this war did not brutalize the hearts of millions of people in this world? And are you going to cure it by brutalizing it still more by capital punishment?

If capital punishment would cure these dire evils that he tells us about, why in the world should there be any more killing? We have had it always. We have had it long enough. It should have been abolished long ago.

In the end, this question is simply one of the humane feelings against the brutal feelings. One who likes to see suffering, out of what he thinks is a righteous indignation, or any other, will hold fast to capital punishment. One who has sympathy, imagination, kindness and understanding, will hate it and detest it as he hates and detests death.

Index